MEMOIRS OF A REDRUTH CHILDHOOD

The Author

Memoirs of a Redruth Childhood

WINIFRED HAWKEY

DYLLANSOW TRURAN

Published by Dyllansow Truran
Trewolsta, Trewirgie, Redruth, Cornwall

© 1987 Winifred Hawkey

Printed and bound in Great Britain
by A. Wheaton & Co. Ltd, Exeter

ISBN 1 85022 024 7

CONTENTS

Pleasures of Memory.

Lull'd in the countless chambers of the brain
Our thoughts are linked by many a hidden chain.

THE DAILY life of a little girl who lived in Redruth, Cornwall, during the early days of this Century.

I was born in Coach Lane, Redruth, on Maundy Thursday, March 27th, 1902, so can claim to have spent the earliest years of my life in the Edwardian era. I have usually celebrated my birthday within the days of the Easter festival, but I had to wait 73 years before it fell on that particular day, as I discovered when I saw a letter in the 'Times' from a gentleman who had been equally deprived. I wrote to him and we corresponded for many years. This year 1986 it will fall on that day, so I have not had to wait so long this time. At any rate I can remember what life was like in a small town before and during the Great War.

I was a very small, puny baby, very much averse to coming into this world, so caused my mother a great deal of pain and trouble, with the result that both she and the 'monthly nurse' were quite worn out with the struggle. I was also evidently very hungry and as my Mother was unable to feed me I was introduced to the bottles which were in use at that time, bottles which were attached to a long rubber tube at the end of which was a teat, a long distance for a weakling baby to suck. I was quite unable to do so, and although I was so tiny my lungs must have been very strong and I used them to some effect, so that, at her wits' end, the nurse said to my parents, "I kent stick this no more. If she d' die don't 'ee tell nobody" and boiled some breakfast biscuits in milk and fed me with a spoon. This had the desired effect. We all slept soundly throughout the night; Mother and the nurse in one room and Daddy and I in the other.

Later the bottle was again offered to me, but I would have none of it, and showed my dislike by throwing it out of my

1

cradle, so that it was broken on the stone floor; and I continued to be fed from a spoon, so I must have survived under this rather unusual treatment as I am now a hale and hearty 84 years old.

One day whilst I was very young, the nurse and Mother took me in a horse-drawn coach to Truro to show me to my grandparents and a fellow traveller, interested as are all women in a new baby, asked the nurse, "Let's have a look at the little 'un. Have 'ee got a boy or a cheeld?" The nurse replied that I was a little girl and was fast asleep. "That don't matter said the lady, "I went wake 'er". Mother was rather surprised that the nurse seemed so reluctant to show me off; but all was revealed when the nurse opened up the shawl and let the interested people in the coach have a look at me, and the lady gasped, and said, "You don't think you're going to rear that do 'ee?" The nurse smoothed my Mother's ruffled plumes by saying severely, "She is a very nice little baby". End of conversation.

I was most elegantly dressed in the fashion of the times. First came a tiny linen 'shirt' which seemed to have no fastenings, but was kept in place by a flannel garment, long and wide, which was wrapped round and tied with numerous tapes. Then came a lawn petticoat trimmed with lace at neck, armholes and hem. The lawn or silk 'long robe' which was put on over all this was very beautiful, trimmed with lace insertion and many tiny tucks. Every little binding at neck, and wrists was 'feather-stitched' and almost all the sewing was done by hand, using tiny needles and '100' cotton, which is almost unobtainable today. Napkins were of Terry towelling, or old soft sheets cut up into squares and hemmed. Disposable diapers were not invented, nor were waterproof panties. Usually, for indoor wear, there was a beautiful shawl, knitted by a kind relation or friend, and these were works of art which, being made of wool, had to be washed very carefully in case they shrank, and were treasured in the family, to be used over and over again, like the elaborate 'christening robe' which is still in evidence today. When carried out we were decked in what was called a 'pelise and cape', made of nun's veiling or some other very fine wool. The 'pelise' part was a long cloak

2

The author at 10 months.

which was wrapped round the baby, and the 'cape' was draped over the carrier's arm. Both parts were trimmed with silk lace and embroidery, and the whole confection looked very grand. I have an example of all of these clothes on a beautiful baby doll, so can describe them in detail; but I can also remember seeing babies so clothed. They did not have much freedom of movement, but must have been much easier to hold.

As soon as I could talk and understand something of what was said to me, Mother taught me to 'say my prayers', kneeling

3

by my bed, each evening. At first I could only ask God to bless all and sundry, with a special mention of relations and kind friends, and say thank you for all the pleasant things in my life (with a little prompting from Mother). Added to this I had to ask Him to make me a good girl, which should have been sufficient even for Mother, but, alas, no, one night I had to add, "Keep me from doing naughty things". I could not think of any dreadful sin I must have committed, and Daddy did not know either when I asked him; but said that if Mother had told me to say it I had better do it, and he expected God would understand. I still have no idea what it could have been. Later she taught me to say, "Gentle Jesus" but it was a long time before I could distinguish between this and all the nursery rhymes I could say. Later when I learned a bit more about Jesus and God I was quite happy about it, as God was a Father like Daddy so it must all be quite easily understood. I always felt quite safe at night, as, as well as God and Jesus looking after me, I could look through the window and see the angels looking down from heaven through the stars; and Daddy and Mother were either downstairs or in the next bedroom, so all was well. We children were fortunate in those days as our lives were uncomplicated, uncluttered and untroubled.

A little later, when I was introduced to corporate worship, I found that very pleasant, too. My godmother's family were Wesleyans, and as I spent much of my time with them I was naturally taken to chapel, where Mrs Paul's God was very kind and forbearing and allowed me to take off my hat if my hair ribbons were sticking into my head, let me sit on a nice soft cushion, and go to sleep if the sermon was long and to me uninteresting. I always woke up to sing the hymns, long before I could read the words, but each Sunday there was one which I had learnt in Sunday School. It was lovely.

But when I was taken to church by Mother, her God was not as nice. I had to sit on a hard chair which was too high for my short legs, kneel for what seemed an unconscionable time on a very thin kneeler, and if I wriggled Mother poked me and looked very cross. But I liked the robed choir and the vestments, and all the other interesting things which seemed to be happening, and after a time could follow the service in my

4

prayer book and also the readings from the Bible, So it all sorted itself out, and I knew I belonged in church as that is where I was baptised, and when I was old enough I should be confirmed and able to accompany the older people to the altar to be blessed and be given help in the taking of the Bread and Wine.

Church Sunday School was nice, too. We learned the catechism, and had it explained to us, and each week we had to recite the collect of the day. Here I was very fortunate. On Saturday mornings, whilst Mother cleaned the stove and scrubbed the floor, she taught me the collect, as she had learned them all and could, with a glance at the prayer book, remember them. So I was 'one up' on my fellow children and was horrid enough to feel proud. But 'pride comes before a fall' as I soon found out. Much later, for scripture homework in school, we had to learn 'The Magnificat,' and I, having said it every Sunday in church, did not bother to look it up, so when asked to recite it set off with assurety, only to be stopped in full flow. I was saying the Prayer Book version, and should have learned the one in the Bible, which is slightly different. Our teacher was a Nonconformist and I was in disgrace. One had to live in Cornwall at that time to realise that Church was Church, and Chapel was Chapel, and neither liked the other very much. I am so glad that today it is all so different, especially as I was equally at home in each, and could never understand why there should be any division, as we all served the same God. I soon realised that Mother's God and Mrs. Paul's were one and the same, and that He didn't mind how we worshipped Him as long as we meant it. In church the services were always the same, so we knew exactly what to join in and where to listen, and children do like everything to go on in the same way, as then they do not find it difficult to conform. It is always the unexpected which upsets them and leaves them wondering 'why' We learned the ten Commandments and our 'duties' from the teaching in Sunday School, so knew exactly how we should live our lives, even if we found it difficult at times. We were given standards so that we knew right from wrong at a very early age, and did try to live up to them, and were sorry and asked God to forgive us if we failed. Life was so settled and

5

comfortable. How fortunate we were. Children today must find everything so difficult to understand when there is so little stability in so many of their lives.

Home and Housework.

THE HOUSE in which we lived in Park Road was not very big, but was most conveniently built, especially for those days; as the ground floor was all on one level, in spite of being on a steep hill; whereas in such a hilly town, most houses were bedevilled with steps both front and back. In the front there were two bay windows, one up and one down, and a smaller window over the front door where my bedroom was situated. We had three bedrooms, a drawing room, a dining room, a kitchen and a scullery, which we called the 'back kitchen'. Because the builder had meant the house for his own family, he had chosen the end position of four houses, so we had a rather larger garden than the others, which was partly why Daddy had chosen it. We were also fortunate to have an indoor toilet, on the half landing, whereas the others had only outdoor flush toilets. This meant that Mother did not have to carry water up to the bedrooms from the back kitchen, as most people had to do. We washed in cold water every day of the year, and each bedroom had, besides a dressing-table, a washstand with a marble top, on which was set a china toilet set, each part of which lay on a mat, either crochetted or made of turkish towelling with knitted lace around the edges. The basin, jug, soapdish and toothbrush container, as well as the chambers, were all decorated with flowers or some other patterns. Mother's were especially pretty, with poppies, cornflowers and ears of corn on them, and the fluted edges were all tipped with gold. Mine was not so elaborate, but I liked it all the same, as Grandpa had brought it for me, as he had the small-sized furniture in light oak.

In my bedroom there were rose buds on the paper, wild roses on the lino and a pink mat on the floor for me to step out on in the morning, and kneel on when I said my prayers. The iron bedstead was painted white, with bits pricked out in gold,

7

all done by Daddy. At the foot of the bed, by the window, stood my bookcase also made by Daddy, and by my bed a sort of cupboard made of an orange box covered in wallpaper and chintz. On this stood my candlestick made of china, and it was also decorated with roses. I still have it, and keep it handy in case of "Power Cuts", which was something we did not have to fear in those days, as we had no electric light in the house; only oil lamps downstairs and candles to light us to bed. My parents had rather elaborate mahogany furniture in their room, whilst that in the spare room was walnut, and here was a wardrobe with a mirror in the door, in front of which I preened myself when dressed in my 'Best' clothes. On the floors of both rooms was linoleum, with here and there warm mats. Edwardian homes abounded in mats of all sorts and sizes, made of every possible material. Some were home-made, like the rag one in the kitchen, and both my bed and that of my parents had bed-spreads made by my Grandma Basset, whom I do not remember. Mine was knitted in white cotton, whilst theirs was made of fanshaped pieces of knitted red and grey wool, sewn together, and both were edged with knitted lace. What a lot of work! Daddy shaved with a cut-throat razor, and I liked to watch him as he lathered his face after sharpening the blade on a leather 'Strop' which hung by the wash-stand. Then he would wipe the razor on a piece of newspaper which I had cut into small squares, and threaded by the corners, before putting them into a sort of cover made of cardboard covered with pink linen. By the dressing-table there hung a similarly coloured 'Hair Tidy'.

Downstairs, back and front, the doorsteps were made of solid blocks of granite, which had to be scrubbed every Saturday so that they shone and sparkled in the sunshine. All granite does so when clean, and that is why the houses in Redruth, which are nearly all built of granite, both gold and grey, look to me much nicer than bricks or plaster. Our hall was tiled in a geometric pattern of blue, brown and white, which also had to be washed each week, though we did not use the front door very often, as to go to town it was much nearer to go down the back lane, as I did with Daddy as he went to shop and I went to catch the train to go to Camborne County School.

Author's Mother   *Author's Father*

The front door had stained glass in the upper part and I can remember a tree with a little bird in it. I believe there were some Italians in the town for a time, as several houses, particularly in our district, had tiled halls. By the wall at the foot of the stairs stood a glass case, and inside was a stuffed fox with a rabbit in its jaws, and some very real-looking blood on its fur. I hated it, and was secretly afraid of it, especially when I had to go upstairs to the lavatory in the half-dark. There was always a light in a little oil lantern hanging in the hall, but this seemed to cast shadows and not help at all. I don't think Mother was enamoured of the fox, either, as she had to dust it and polish the glass. Perhaps Daddy was not all that fond of it either. It may have been a wedding-present, and was certainly a good example of the taxidermist's art. Anyway, one day it disappeared, and when I asked what had become of it, Mother said she had 'Sent it down the Salesroom', as she did with anything which she did not like. We did not use the dining room much as it was warmer in the kitchen and much sunnier. In winter the range kept it warm and there were two easy chairs as well as the ones we sat on for meals. On Sundays,

9

when there was more time to sit and read or sew, Mother lit the fire in the drawing room and we sat there. Later, when I was at the County School and had so much home-work to do, I sat alone in the dining room with a big lamp to keep me warm, and could work uninterrupted from after tea until bed-time. I was very fortunate that I could do this, as many of my friends who had brothers and sisters were unable to have so much time to themselves.

I think modern housewives have no idea of the amount of work our mothers had to do. There were no labour-saving appliances or any other sort of help. All had to be done by hand with cloths, brushes and 'elbow grease'. Mondays seemed to be the worst day in the week, as everywhere it was "Washday". Mother did employ Mrs. Whitford to do the bulk of it. With no washing machines or spin driers everything had to be rubbed by hand and the drying left to the vagaries of the weather, often unreliable in our neck of the woods. On Sunday mornings Mother used to put the dirty clothes in a big galvanised bath to soak. She rubbed them with some sort of soap which had parafin in it, supposed to loosen the dirt. This presented some hazards, as Daddy and Grandpa had an air-gun, and used to practise with it in the kitchen. They put the paper targets on the wall, and so as not to make holes in the plaster or wall paper, they piled heaps of this soap behind them, with the result that as Mother was rubbing she often came upon little pellets; but that did not deter her from using the soap. It was too dear to waste.

On Monday morning, Daddy used to get up very early, fill the boiler in the scullery with cold water, light the fire under it, and turn the table on to its side to make it lower, as Mrs. Whitford was very short. We say she 'lacked the inches', which is very expressive. She came every Monday to do the washing, and for this received the princely sum of one shilling, her breakfast, dinner and tea, and other things to take home with her, such as food or half worn clothing. For breakfast she always had a boiled egg, and I, who at no other time could be induced to eat an egg, enjoyed a taste off her spoon, to Mother's dismay; but she was powerless to do anything about it lest she offended the dear old soul, who was very fond of me

10

and let me 'help' her and get in the way as much as I liked. Mother grew accustomed to having to put me into dry clothes when this performance was over, as I was naturally as wet as the clothes I 'washed'. Sometimes I produced dolls' clothes and these went in with the rest. She must have been very good-tempered, kindly, soul as I must have been a real hindrance. The payment seems to us to be a dreadfully mean amount, but it was the 'going' pay at the time, and she liked coming to us as Daddy did not have a 'dirty' job, and Mother always deterred me from getting in a mess if she possibly could. In some of the houses where she went to work the family was much bigger and the clothes much dirtier. She always had 'washerwoman's hands' wrinkled and white and sad-looking, poor little soul. I am glad people do not have to do much for so little today. When washed, rinsed and put through the big mangle with its wooden rollers, the clothes could be pegged out on the lines Daddy had put up before going to work. Nearly all the clothes could be mangled in those days as the buttons were linen, an did not break as the plastic ones do. The Mother-of-pearl ones were only on best clothes, and these Mother did herself by hand. We had a neighbour who lived in the top house and who got up very, very early on Mondays; so that when Daddy was putting up the lines, she would call down to him, "Washed, dried and ironed and baked bread and cake." It was a sort of regular joke between them, and one Sunday evening Daddy put a teatowel on the line, and in the morning said, "Beat you today". We all had a good laugh over it and it remained our special bit of fun until Daddy and Mother left Redruth. We were all happy together in Park Road, all good neighbours ready to help each other whenever help was needed.

After all the washing was done, there was still the fire to be raked out, the copper to dry and the table and floor to be scrubbed. I believe, too, the remainder of the warm soapy water was used to scrub the outside lavatory, seat and floor, and to swill down the drains. I feel sure that every Monday could not have been a fine day with a good 'Drieth up', but I do not remember wet clothes lying around. When dry they would be taken in, folded and again put through the mangle, and those needing ironing put aside until Tuesday. As Mother always starched the linen tablecloth and dinner napkins, as well as some of my frilly clothes, there was a lot of ironing, and all the starched things had to be damped down before they could be ironed. Daddy's white collars had to be done with cold-water starch, which is hard to iron as it likes to stick to the iron. My Godmother's husband wore a starched 'dicky' in the front of his shirts, as well as starched cuffs, and I liked watching Mrs. Paul doing these. They had to be very shiny when finished and she used to bend the cuffs and the neck bits of the 'dicky' so that they would be comfortable as well as smart when worn. Mother did Daddy's collars, but she did not look so deft as Mrs. Paul. She had not so much practise, as she did not have three sons as well as a husband to look after. Most people ironed on the kitchen table, which was not easy as the backs and fronts of shirts etc. could not be spread out. Daddy saw Mother using a board with one end on the table and the other on the back of a chair, so he made her an ironing-board, a folding one in shape like those sold today, but in wood and much more stable. He made me one too, when I got married, and I still use it. Until Daddy made Mother's we had never seen anything like it. Ironing was a very hot tiring job: there were of course no electric irons. The ones used were of two sorts. There was a 'flat' iron which was a smooth triangle of iron with a handle attached. It was heated on the top of the range. Then there was what was called a 'box heater' which is exactly what it was. There was a wedge shaped box of iron with a brass base. In it were inserted other wedge shaped pieces of iron pre-heated in the fire. The 'box' had a sort of door in the broad end, with a handle with which to lift it up and down, and through this the heated piece of iron was inserted. If there was a lot of ironing to do the inside had to be changed very often to keep it at the right heat; so the poor ironer had always to be by the stove and got very hot and tired. It was a long time before we had gas in our house, and then Mother had a gas iron; but that was clumsy and a bit dangerous, as there was a flame inside the box and it might have caught the clothes afire. Not until she came to live in Plymouth did Mother ever have an electric iron, and even then steam ones had not come on the market.

The only form of heating throughout the houses was by coal

fires. In the sitting rooms and bedrooms there were iron grates which when used had to be raked out each morning and relaid with paper, chopped wood and small lumps of coal, to coax the fire to light before the larger lumps could be added. These grates had to be blackleaded. At first I remember Mother using some very messy blacklead which had to be moistened with water or vinegar and then the specially shaped brush was dipped into the container (usually an old saucer) applied to the grate, taking special care to go between the many bars, and then the whole polished until it shone, with a second brush. All these utensils lived in a sort of wooden basket with a handle, so that they could be easily taken from one room to another. We had a fire in the bedroom only if ill, and that meant that the coal etc. had to be carried from the coalhouse, outside the back door, up all the stairs.

Each morning the grate of the kitchen range had to be cleared out and relaid so that the fire could be lighted to boil the kettle for the first cup of tea, which Daddy brought up to Mother and me. When we had Kitty Whiskers she used to have a drop of mine in my saucer. In the summer Daddy would boil the kettle on the primus, but like all the oil lamps which gave us light, this too had to be cleaned or it would not function properly. The lamps, like the range, were an everyday job, there was no shrinking either of them.

All cooking had to be done in the oven of the range or on its top. The oven regularly got 'sooted' up and it was Daddy's job on some Thursday afternoons to take it out into the garden and brush off all the soot, otherwise Mother would not have been able to bake in it. I naturally very much wanted to assist, but even Daddy said, "No," and I had to be content to watch through the back-kitchen window.

After this I was removed to the front of the house whilst he cleaned out the part where the oven lived, and more soot had congregated. Naturally this was an even dirtier job which Mother was glad did not have to be done very often, as she was left to wash off all the soot which had spread everywhere, no matter how careful Daddy had been. Daddy's job too, was to wash the windows. He had a whitewash brush with the head set at rightangles, fixed onto two broom handles so that it could reach up to the top windows, and he squirted water up to the panes with a syringe. It was my delight to stand inside each window in turn, so that he could squirt the water at me and pretend to make me wet. Then as he washed the glass with the brush it was fun to point out any bit he had missed.

All the windows in the front of the house had Venetian blinds, the slats made of wood and painted green. They had to be brushed and dusted each week, and at Spring Cleaning time they were taken down repainted, or washed and polished. Sometimes the webbing had rotted and had to be renewed. Then they were hung up to the rafters in the scullery and each slat had to be done separately, a long fiddling job, but I liked it as I could help, and if very good was allowed to do a bit of painting. I never thought about it, but I suppose the paint faded because our house must have faced due South. The back windows looked right over the the North Coast, and the kitchen window, which was on the side, to the West and Carn Brea.

Each week every room was cleaned. I was supposed to help with my own little room as well as in the others, I am afaid I was not much help really, as I was not a very consistent worker. As soon as I started dusting my bookcase I stopped to read something, and had often to be recalled to the job in hand. It was better to give me something in another part of the house. There were many other things that needed doing. For one thing there were no stainless steel knives. Ours were all made of fine Sheffield steel, sharp and I suppose a bit dangerous to clean. But they did cut which is more than can be said of most of those we have to use today. Thank goodness we have three of the old ones still in use, and they are veritable treasures, better than any gadget I have yet tried to use. To clean them we had to rub them up and down on a knife board, a piece of wood covered with leather, on which we sprinkled very fine emery powder. If one of them was badly stained it was a 'good bright' to cut a potato in half, dip it in the powder, and then rub it on the blade of the knife. Afterwards of course one had to rub particularly hard to make it shine again. The spoons and forks which we used were silver plated and they stained very easily, so had to be polished every week. To do this we used pink plate powder which we put in a saucer and made into a paste with cold water. Then we dipped a soft rag into this concoction and rubbed the spoons and forks with it. Our hands got very dirty and it was a horrid job which I hated, but Mother was not satisfied until there was a good shine on every one. The forks were the worst, as I had to be sure to go between every prong and it hurt my nails. Besides these everyday ones, Mother had a special "posh" set which she and Daddy had bought in London when on their honeymoon. I thought this was very romantic, but wished they had chosen a plainer pattern. These were of the "king" pattern and had many indentations up the handles, and a shell at the end. To get into all the grooves I had to use a special brush, and was secretely very glad that they were used only on special occasions. These treasures spent most of their time wrapped in chamois leather in the dining room sideboard.

On Saturdays after the kitchen had been 'done' as I have already explained, the staircarpet had to be brushed down and the stair-rods polished. This was not so bad, as they were straight little brass rods which presented no problems, and were really quite nice to do, pushing each one up and down in my hand and seeing the shining part coming out at each end, something to show for one's work. In both sittingrooms we had carpets which had to be brushed. Mother put tea leaves down to collect the dust, but still some rose up around the furniture and it was my job to remove this. It was not a very hard thing to do but the chairs and tables had fluted legs, and Mother was very particular that I did not miss any bit. I forgot to say that the upholstered easy chairs had to have the same treatment as the carpets, so this also made dust on the legs. Upstairs the floors were covered with linoleum which had to be washed, and the rugs by the beds, washstands and dressing tables had to be taken down into the garden to be shaken and brushed.

I was not very fond of washing dishes, but as I was usually given only the tea things it was not so bad. Most of the saucepans were made of iron for use on the range and so were heavy, but we also had a 'primus' oil lamp to use in the summer, if the range was not lit, and on that Mother used enamel ones. When using them one had to be careful that the

15

food did not stick in the bottom as they were rather thin. Before the war Mother always laid the table properly, vegetable dishes, sauce boat and all, but during the war the amount of food was much less and she then served it straight from the saucepans, and there was not always a joint for Daddy to carve, which he had always done. I never saw a lady carve a joint until I left home. Mother was very particular about table manners even when I was quite small and I am horrified nowadays when I see how people who ought to know better hold their knives and forks. Our cups and saucers were always made of china, whereas many people used 'cloam' (earthenware) as it did not break so easily, but Mother would not drink out of a thick cup. the result was that when I washed the dishes I had to be very careful not to pour very hot water onto them as that would have cracked them, and there could never be the time-honoured excuse 'that it came away in my hand'. But another result is that I do not like thick crockery either.

The highlight or rather the nadir of any housewife's year was 'spring cleaning'. Then everything in the house had to "go through it". Not a spot was neglected, no matter how much out of sight it was. Mother had been taught that if one cleaned the corners the middle would take care of itself; which is not so ridiculous after all, as when all the corners have been turned out, the middle is in such a muddle that one simply has to tidy it. The first thing to be thought of was to order the sweep to clear the chimneys of soot which had accumulated through the year. There were of course no 'vac' sweeps as there was no electricity so it was important to employ a sweep who was known to be a "clean" one, for no matter how careful he was the soot seemed to fly everywhere so one always tried to get one recommended by a friend, or one whom you knew from past experience. In fact most of the people who worked for us were thought of as friends, as the same people came to the house year after year and were very well known to us. I can remember only one postman and one milkman all the time I lived in Redruth.

Before the "Day" there was an awful lot to do in preparation. All the bigger pieces of furniture had to be brushed, polished and covered in wrappers, whilst all moveable objects were taken out of the room, the ornaments to be washed, the pictures to be washed and polished, and the small chairs and tables to be given an extra polish. Then the carpets were taken up and put on the clothes-line, to be beaten with a special beater made of cane, and Daddy's walking stick for good measure. I liked doing this, especially if I was allowed to go under the two halves of the carpet and pretend I was an Arab in his tent. The winter curtains were taken down to have their turn at being cleaned later, and the Nottingham lace ones taken out to be starched and ironed. If you have never had to iron such curtains you have missed one of the most frustrating jobs in the world. They just WILL NOT go straight, no matter how hard you pull and struggle. They usually had to be put up a bit out of true, and we had to wait for them to settle down on their own. Thank goodness for nylon! All the walls in those days were papered, and downstairs had picture rails above which there was usually a very pretty frieze. I remember that the one in the drawingroom was a light blue, with pretty little birds on it. I sometimmes tried to count them, but always got tired before I got all round the room. Some years a room had to be re-papered, and Daddy and I had fun before it was done, writing each other letters on the old paper, and drawing all sorts of things. I liked to help scrape off the paper when it had been wetted, a messy job, perhaps that is why I liked it. I could get dirty without being scolded. I helped with the new paper, too, the paste was made of flour and water and was lovely and sticky.

After the sweep had gone Mother always scrubbed the floor and made the wood as white as the kitchen table, before putting down the carpet and replacing all the furniture etc. It did look nice, and smelled so sweet that we thought all the hard work had been worth it. Even I could appreciate it.

Another thing I liked doing was to tidy all the drawers, as then I usually turned out something I had forgotten, but it was not so pleasant if Mother decided that it could be got rid of as it was no longer used. Even if I had not been interested in it before, immediately I thought it was to disappear I wanted it, but Mother was not easily moved by my coaxing or even tears,

17

so out it went. Opposite our house there were no other houses, only the gardens of the houses in Clinton Road, and in them were several fir trees in which rooks made their nests every year. Their ceaseless cawing was not appreciated by any one in the road, but nobody thought that anything could be done about it. Daddy did. One night he opened the bedroom window, stuck his double-barrelled gun out and fired into the trees. It frightened the rooks and some of them went away, but it frightened the neighbours too, though they never knew where the shot came from. So you see that although I was always busy I was also interested, and happy nearly all the time.

Mother was very determined that I should be a good girl, but she was never unkind, and my punishments were always very mild ones, easily borne, especially as I usually realised that I had earned them. She even put up with me getting dirty when I 'helped' Daddy. It was especially so when we whitewashed the back kitchen, I had a little brush all of my own and 'did the low bits, and myself, but it all came out in the wash and kept me happy.

Every Day Happenings

ALTHOUGH I was an only child I do not remember ever feeling lonely or bored, and I am sure I could always find something to do by myself. Of course I cannot remember how I amused myself when very young, but I have been assured by my Mother that I was always 'busy', often to the detriment of my immediate surroundings; but as that happens to all babies as soon as they can crawl, mothers learn to expect it. Very early in life I attached myself to my father and wanted to 'help' him in whatever he was doing. Once when he was planting potatoes I tried to pull them up as fast as he put them in, so he resolved the problem by 'planting' me at the beginning of each row, leaving me there to play with the earth and look for 'wollums' while he got on with the rest of the row. I became very dirty but was quite happy. Mother has also told me that I was very fond of sitting under the tap outside the backdoor, especially if it had not been turned off properly and dripped.

Just before I was two years old we moved to Park Road into a house called Linden House, why, I haven't a notion, as there wasn't a lime tree anywhere in the vicinity. My parents bought the house as Mother's Mother had died and left her £100 and with this and their savings they were able to do so. My Grandmother had contracted cancer when I was six months old and whilst she was so ill my Mother often went to Truro to look after her and I was 'parked' on my Godmother, Mrs. Paul, whose husband was the cutter in the outfitting shop where Daddy was manager. Their family consisted of three boys and two girls, all much older than I, though Lily, the youngest, was only ten, and thought that I was her special property. They all treated me as one of the family and I was always happy with them. Lily spent much time with me, and when I cried and Mother said I was so naughty she would 'send me back', Lily would say, "Don't send her back please, I will take her for a little walk and she will be quite good when we come home again". She could not bear to think of losing me. As I grew older I was torn between wanting a baby sister of my own and at the same time dreading it, as Mother, when I was naughty, threatened to send for one, and added, "Then your Daddy won't love you anymore" This was something I could not face. It was so awful that I did not even ask Daddy if it was true, though in my heart of hearts I could not believe it. I wish I had told him of my fears, as then he would have allayed them, but somehow I never did, and for many years this fear was always with me. It was a strange threat to use, and perhaps it was just as well that the little girl never materialised.

Daddy bred field spaniels, and my best loved friend and constant companion was 'Champion Linden Monogram', our dear 'Monnie' with whom my childhood photos were taken. She won numerous prizes in the local show as well as in the more important ones. The local ones were given by the Redruth photographer, and as my long fair hair and best frilly frock contrasted with the shining black coats of the dogs, I was always included. When I look at these pictures now I feel joy, and sadness that they are no longer here to be loved. Nowadays when I see 'Cruft's' on the television I get very angry watching the owners holding up their dogs' tails, and pulling up their heads with a lead, running round nearly choking them. In our days when a dog was 'shown' she either jumped on the bench or was lifted there, and then was left alone to show herself. We did not go near — let alone touch her. I know this as when Daddy could not get time off to go to the show, Mother and I went instead, which was quite alright as Monnie and Melody, our black and tan bitch, knew exactly what was expected of them. Once when Mother tried to look over the judge's shoulder to see what he was writing he said, "You needn't look, Mrs. Hawkey — nobody could find fault with your dog". In those days too, no sporting dog could win a championship unless he or she had been 'short over', that is, having been out with a strange shooting party and shown that she knew exactly what was expected of her. Monnie was quite happy in this test as she always went with Daddy when he

20

Humphrey T. Williams – Outfitters, Fore Street, Redruth,
where the author's father was manager.

went shooting on his brother's or cousin's farms. When I look
at them now having every hair put in place whilst actually on
the bench I feel sure that any one of them would run a mile if a
shot was fired near them.

Daddy came from a farming family and should have been a
vet and not a draper at all, as he really hated that way of
earning a living; but Grandma had a large family to bring up all
by herself as Grandpa had died, and she decided what each
one should do, and in those days young people did what they
were told whether they liked it or not. Daddy's brother, my
Uncle Willie, who was a farmer, had the same gift with animals
and was always called in when any animal on a near-by farm
was 'off colour' and needed assistance. In Redruth anybody
who had a pet which showed signs of being off colour brought

21

it to Daddy, who always seemed to be able to make it well again, or rear any weaklings in a family. As I was always with him, I grew up without any fear of animals at all, and was able to carry on the treatment whilst he was at work. At one time I remember that Mrs. Tom Trounson had some fantailed pigeon nestlings whose mother neglected them, so Daddy brought them home. As they had to have their food moistened with saliva and chewed very fine, we softened it in our mouths and fed them from our lips. It was a very slow job, but was worth it, because the fledglings grew to be lovely pigeons. Fortunately nobody had a tame snake, as I am sure I should have disliked it very much, but should have had to do my best for it! We had at one time or another almost every kind of animal, and I was very glad I was able to help them back to active life. As Daddy often went to Allet near Truro, where the family farms were, he kept two ferrets in a cosy box in the outside lavatory. When Mother sent me there to 'be a good girl' I used to put my hand into the box and take out one of them for company. They were accustomed to being handled and when out rabbiting they lived in Daddy's 'poacher's pocket'. Not that he went poaching as he had a game licence and could shoot on any of his relations' farms. This pocket was very useful for all sorts of things, as when we were out together it could hold food or fishing tackle or even a doll if I wanted one with me. Miss Shy Nail (of whom more later) had many a ride in it. All went well with the ferrets and me until Mother found out, and she was horrified in case they bit me, so I was forbidden to handle them, which was really silly as they never would have done so, as, I had no fear. I then had to open the box and explain to my little friends why I could no longer fondle them when they were in their box. Of course I could still do so when they were in Daddy's pocket. I am sure animals know instinctively when there is no fear and respond to affection. I have never been hurt by any animal, and I am sure there must have been occasions when it could have happened had I been afraid.

I had Monnie for company as soon as I could walk and sometimes her puppies as well. Some time later Mother and Daddy cycled out to Tregavethan Manor, where Auntie Emma and Uncle Josiah lived, and Mother brought home a tiny tabby kitten cuddled up warm inside her blouse. I can remember Daddy feeding her with some minced beef tied up in muslin so that she could suck it. I suppose she was really very young to be taken from her mother; but she must have learned to lap very quickly as she grew to be a very handsome cat. She probably had a much nicer life with us than she would have had on the farm, as she was loved by us all. Monnie treated her as if she was her puppy, and so provided the warmth etc. which she would have got from her mother, and we fed her with many things she would not have had on the farm. She liked being fondled and played with. Sad to relate though, she must have gone out courting and was to have kittens of her own; and as at that time birth was a forbidden subject, Mother decided that she must be "killed". I use that horrid word intentionally as there was no easy 'putting to sleep' as we can have done to our much loved pets nowadays, there was only drowning or poison. I still hate to think of what happened to poor 'Kitty Whiskers' — Mother told me that she had got lost, and I hunted for her all over the place for a long time, and worried what had befallen her, imagining all sorts of horrible accidents or thinking of her wandering cold and hungry, unable to find her way home to us. If only Mother had said that she had gone to Heaven to play with the Angels, I should still have missed her, but should have been spared all that misery, for I am sure that I did not tell anyone, not even Daddy, of all the things I imagined.

Perhaps here is the place to explain that in my childhood and youth I had no knowledge of sex at all. There were of course mothers and fathers, boys and girls, uncles and aunties, and on the farms, cows and bulls, hens and cockerels, horses and mares, but it never occurred to me to wonder at the different names. I was quite sure that all the baby things came straight from God, and that Angels brought them down from Heaven, usually in the night; those same Angels who kept watch over us whilst we slept, looking down on us through those chinks in the sky which we called stars. Of course all tiny things had to be kept warm, and that was why their mothers kept them close to their sides and fed them. This idea that we all come from God is perhaps not foolish after all. Wordsworth evidently

23

thought so. He wrote, 'Not in entire forgetfullness and not in utter nakedness, but trailing clouds of Glory do we come from God, who is our Home. Heaven lies about us in our infancy'. If that is true there can be no fear of death, we only return to God whence we came.

Later our dear Monnie became old and had some form of skin disease, and Mother decided that it was not healthy for me to spend so much time with her and that Daddy must 'get rid of her'. I can hardly bear, even now, to think about it. I feel sure though that Daddy must have shot her himself, rather than let her suffer the dreadful pain of poison. She was so dear to us. I cannot imagine how he must have suffered. We never mentioned it at the time, but once when he was very old he said to me, "Your Mother need not have got rid of the dear old dog. You would not have caught anything from her". I just said, "I know Daddy", and we just sat and were sad together. It is something I would rather forget than remember, but we cannot control our memories. We have to ' mind' things good or bad, we have no choice. Perhaps that is a good thing. When Daddy was very old he once said to me, "One of the compensations of getting old is that you can live over again things which happened in the past, and can take as long as you like over them. I have had many a good day's sport since I have been sitting here and I can take my time enjoying them". That is true, but all memories cannot be undiluted joy, and the sad ones are the ones we must keep from poking their heads up. Daddy and I always did things together, so it was only natural that we should feel happiness and sadness together.

Besides being a champion and winning prizes, Monnie was our faithful friend and the best of guard dogs. She did not bark or show her teeth, but whenever Mother went to answer the door Monnie always preceded her, and stood quietly in front of her, ready to look after her if need arose. She let me cuddle her puppies as much as I liked, and one day Daddy found me washing each on in a dipper. When asked what I was up to this time, I replied that I was 'bashing em'. Daddy explained that I must not do it as they might catch cold, and that Monnie herself would keep them clean. I expect they were really very valuable puppies but Daddy did not scold me, and Monnie

24

saved them from harm but did not do anything to stop me. She never hurt anyone in all her life. She was always to be trusted.

The people who lived in our house before Daddy and Mother bought it had a pony and trap, so at the bottom of our garden there was a stable and a coach house. Daddy turned the stable into a sort of nursery for the dogs and their babies, and the coach house he left empty as a run for them in bad weather. He also fenced off a part of that end of the garden so that they could have a run when the weather was fine. Much later when we had lost Monnie, and Daddy did not want to keep any other dog, he cleaned up the coach house to make a playroom for me. It was lovely, with rugs on the floor, curtains at the window, and in it I had an old wickerwork chair, a little stool, a dolls' house he had made for me, and some of my toys and dolls — whichever I decided to take down with me whenever Mother wanted me out of the way. I was always pleased to go there as I could do what I liked and not make a mess in the house. Sometimes some of my friends came to play with me and they all looked forward to playing in 'Winnie's Dogs' House'. There we could do as we liked. We played all sorts of imaginative games and 'pretended' all kinds of entertainments, with no fear of having to stop and put everything away before we finished. But I was really a tidy little girl and kept my 'house' clean and nice all the time. This itself was a game to me and I enjoyed doing it. The wooden roof was almost covered with the cards showing all the prizes which the dogs had won and I often read them upside down and thought about each dog which had gained each prize. Alone, my imagination knew no bounds: I played 'shops' or 'schools' with my dolls, and made them beautiful birthday cakes out of mud, icing them with lime out of Daddy's bucket, and decorating them with flowers from the garden. I had two dolls' teasets; one was made with blue enamel like the saucepans, and other was a beautiful china one which I never took into the Dogs' House in case I let any part fall to break in pieces on the cement floor. It was very elegant, having plates as well as cups and saucers, and a large cake plate. It was decorated with pink roses and had too, of all things — a fruit bowl. I have no idea what became of it but I still had some of the enamel one after I was married and all the

25

children who came to tea had it to play with.

I once had a wax doll, but her face melted when I put her by the fire, I was not very upset. I did not like her very much, she simpered. Two very nice ladies who lived near Grandpa in Roskear, on the way to Camborne, gave me three really beautiful dolls with 'bisque' porcelain faces and jointed limbs. One was a dark beauty with ebony curls. She wore a blue satin dress and bonnet and lovely underclothes trimmed with lace, and all her clothes could be taken off. That is essential if any doll is to be played with. Unfortunately a little friend who came to tea dropped her on the kitchen floor, and her poor face and body broke into so many pieces that she could not be mended. She did not have a name as I had had her for only a few days, so did not feel too sorry when she was broken. Another was a blonde beauty with a sweet face and even jointed wrists. She had (and still has) a white silk frock with tiny tucks and lace insertion, and her underclothes are just as elegant as were those of the first doll. She was able to wear the dark doll's clothes as well as her own, and I made a lot more for her. She is called Esmé Joyce and one of my God-daughters has her now — but most of those lovely clothes are missing, mother probably gave them away. I knitted her a pair of stockings with a properly turned heel and grafted toes. I had no very fine wool so I used mending wool and very long darning needles, with the result that I got very pricked fingers; but these have gone the way of all her other clothes. Mother was very good at getting rid of things which to her were of little importance. She had a mania for Sales Rooms and we never knew what would be the next to go. Once when I went home, I missed a little folding chair of which I was very fond I asked Daddy where it was and he said mother had sent it down to the sales room. I said,"Oh why did you let her do that?", and he answered that he had looked at the list and as his name wasn't on it he thought he had better not say a word. Bless him! He could always make a joke of everything that was not really serious.

The third was a baby doll dressed exactly as a real baby would have been at that time. When it has its bonnet on it is a girl, but when the bonnet is taken off it becomes a boy with a little kiss curl on his forehead, so he/she is called Lesley which does for either. Once mother was carrying him home for me on the tram-car and a woman opposite said, 'Fancy bringing the dear cheel out at this time of night, you ought to be ashamed of yourself! Tis time the poor li'l toad was 'ome in bed', and was most amused when Mother showed that it was a doll she was carrying and not a real baby. My other God-daughter has Lesley now. He had a loose arm from being so much loved and I took him to a dolls' hospital to be mended. When it was done the proprietress told me that he is very valuable and should be kept in a cupboard and not be played with any more, but I am sure he would not like that. He is not accustomed to being shut away, as there is always another generation ready to love him.

But my liking for these beauties paled before my abiding love for 'Miss Shy Nail', a rag doll made up for me from a printed sheet which had been sent to Shop as an advertisement. The girls in the workroom had sewn her for me and she was stuffed with cut up pieces left over from things they were making at the time. I do not know how old I was when first I had her, she seemed to have been there always. She was not particularly beautiful in other people's eyes, but to me she was perfect; my 'alter ego', the sister I never had, the companion of all my days and nights. I loved her more than anyone except Mother and Daddy, told her all my troubles (I can't see why unless it seemed to me to be suitable as her face was so dirty) and dressed her in my cast-off clothes. Once Mother washed her and put her out to dry and a puppy we had 'minding' at that time, found her and tore her up. I found her, and rushed in to Mother crying, "She's deaded, she's deaded". So Mother had to stop whatever she was doing and sew her together again, as I cried and cried until she was safely back in my arms. We played all sorts of games together: Ludo, Snakes and Ladders, and all sorts of card games, and if she won too often to please me I put her down under the bed to punish her, but very soon took her out again and kissed her to show she was forgiven. It is very hard for an only child to learn how to lose. Brothers and sisters soon knock the corners off one, but without any siblings one has to learn all by oneself. It is absolutely necessary to do so, as otherwise one would not be able to take one's place in the world; but it takes time and I think it was made easier for me

27

when I realised that one cannot remain out of temper with any loved one for any length of time. It was so with Miss Shy Nail — I could not remain cross with her. I could not bear it.

By now I should have explained how she got her extraordinary name. The printed linen came from a firm named, 'The Shynall Rag Company'. At last her face, patch and all, really wore out; so Lily Paul made her a new one out of flannelette which could be put on over her real one, but it had to be made with a drawstring so that I could take it off each night, kiss her 'Good night' and then put it on again. She was indeed a real part of me, so much so that when I came home from my first term at the University and found that she was not on by bed waiting for me to tell her all about it, I felt somehow deprived, and asked Mother what had become of her, only to be told that she had been given away to Gladys Wills. I had always given everything I could spare to Gladys, and she could have had anything else, but Miss Shy Nail was something different, something very precious, and deep down I never really forgave Mother for giving her away when I was not there to rescue her. Many years later, when I spoke to Gladys about her, she — dear simple soul, understood, and said exactly the right thing. 'Don't 'ee worry Miss Winnie, she was dearly loved'.

All my other pastimes were as nothing to my love of books. Before I had learned to talk properly I greeted each newcomer to the house with the demand, 'Weed to me', and produced a book. At first I saw only the pictures but very soon demanded so much attention that I found that I must learn to read by myself; not only the Beatrix Potter stories which I could read 'upside down', (as I knew them by heart), but real stories where the pictures were only there to assist those whose imaginations needed stimulating, and the text was what really mattered. Soon I demanded longer and longer stories, and although I could still enjoy Peter Rabbit and his friends, I progressed to Francis Hodgson Burnett and 'The Little Princess', 'Little Lord Fauntleroy' and 'The Secret Garden', all of which told real stories (and were beautifully written). I cried over 'Black Beauty' and another equally heartrending tale of 'Beautiful Joe' in which a dog was maltreated but turned out to be a very brave and well-loved pet. I think it is no longer published, which is a pity, especially when you think of the dreadful suffering some inflict on harmless animals. Every time I re-read Black Beauty I feel so glad that horses are no longer used on our roads. I had 'Annuals' as they came out, not many in those days, but I remember one special one published by 'Blackie's' in a lovely blue binding and can even remember some of the stories in it. Of course I went through the 'Comic' stage and had 'The Rainbow' each week. In Redruth we had a 'Pasmore Edwards' Free Library, a God-send to all avid readers who could not afford to buy books. The librarian was to me, a little old man with whiskers, who looked formidable, but was really very kind and knew exactly which books we should read according to our age or ability. He led me carefully through the stages, first with all the Andrew Lang book of fairy stories, each volume having a colour to recognise it by, then came Hans Anderson, but not Grimms until I was old enough not to be frightened by the horrors in their books — I lapped them up later. Then came the 'Katy' stories, 'Pollyanna', 'Rebecca', 'Anne of Green Gables', and after them, 'Rewards and Fairies', 'Puck of Pook's Hill', 'Alice', 'The Water Babies', 'The Jungle Books', the 'Just So Stories', 'Gulliver's Travels' and 'Westward Ho'. When we came to Dickens I am ashamed to say that I did not like many of them although I did enjoy 'Oliver Twist' and 'David Copperfield'. I could not wade through the others, but strange to tell, I enjoyed all Scott's novels, in spite of their inordinate length. I am grateful to this gentleman for guiding my literary footsteps, as later on when I had to study these same books, they came to me as old friends. As I grew older I acquired a catholic taste in literature, and I am sure that what I read in my early years led me on to the enjoyment of our greatest heritage — 'Good English'. I was also fortunate that friends never had to wonder what to give me as presents, they could always find a book, and as I was home from school so often with bronchities, I had plenty of time to enjoy reading. Sometimes when Mother wanted to get rid of me for a time, or thought I needed punishing for something, she would send me to bed. But that was never a punishment as I had all my books in a bookcase which Daddy had made for me, at the foot of my bed, so I could read to my heart's content. Once when I was very little and was in bed poorly, Daddy came up to read to me. Mother hearing the sound of sobs, came to see what was the matter, only to be told by me, amid sobs. 'Don't stop, don't stop. I am having a lovely time'. I still think that the way to enjoy a book is to lose oneself in the story. Daddy was reading to me some of Mother's childhood books, 'Tim's Troubles' or 'City Sparrows' or, most tear-jerkingly of all, 'Ada and Gerty — or Hand in Hand Heavenward'. Anyone who can remain unmoved by unhappiness in a book cannot be what an old friend of mine called 'feeling hearted', and that I certainly was, and am still. When Mother was old and could no longer see to read, I used to read aloud to her almost every afternoon, and when we came to a moving passage we both had to stop to wipe our eyes before we could go on again. Daddy used to read to me very often, taking me on his knee and reading one of my favourites. When he thought he had had enough, he would suggest that he read some of his books instead. I thought it quite fair that we should each have a turn, and he would read out of a catalogue of seeds or plants, and I am sure that I acquired a lot of horticultural knowledge in this way, though of course I did not realise it at the time.

In those days many houses had big screens to keep out draughts which came under the doors or from ill-fitting windows, and these screens were often decorated with 'scraps' or pictures cut out of magazines, or sometimes picture post-cards. We did not have a screen, but I made 'scrapbooks' for my little friends. We could buy for a penny a page of such 'scraps', each picture having a serrated edge for easy separation. Each sheet was composed of pictures of one subject, such as flowers, animals etc. and it was fun to arrange them. The glue was messy but we did not mind getting our fingers sticky and our Mothers made sure that we had spread newspaper on the table before we started. Some clever people sometimes painted their own pictures, but I could never aspire to that. Although my fingers would do anything I asked of them with a needle, or a crochet hook, or even two or four knitting needles, they refused to do anything in the way of drawing or painting.

Sometimes I helped Mother turn sides to the middle of a worn sheet or make under-pillow slips of the better parts, and 'cold' handkies from the very worn soft bits, (these were very acceptable for sore noses as they were absorbent as well as being very soft). Of course by this time I had learned to use her sewing machine and in school had learned to 'darn'. We wore long black woollen stockings and they often got torn, especially at the knee if we fell down on the rough roads. Once I told Mother that she had not darned my stocking very tidily, whereupon she told me that if I was not satisfied I could in future do them myself, and from that day on I had to do so. It was suprising how careful I was not to fall down or tear any part of my stockings after that. I found it much easier to grow a new bit of knee than to darn a big hole even with the help of the mushroom shaped piece of wood provided.

Sometimes I went next-door to play with Gwennie Earl who was not much older than I. She had three much older sisters and the eldest, Minnie, had to keep house and look after her sisters as their father had died and their mother was keeping the printing business at the top of Station Hill (it's still there). Minnie ruled us not with a 'rod of iron', but with a toasting fork! She sat at the head of the table and if either of us annoyed her she cracked the victim's knuckles with the toasting-fork, so you can be assured we tried to behave. It must have been a hard job for her as she was only a teenager herself, but there was no help from the Government for 'one parent families' in those days, and a widow had to look after her children as best she could, so Mrs. Earl ran the business and Minnie had to take on the mantle of homemaker.

I also went to the third house in Park Road where lived an older couple who had come home from California. They had lost their own little girl, called Emmie, from tuberculosis, and as I was a careful little soul I was allowed to play with her toys and read her books. Sometimes Mr. Trengrove played 'Ludo' with me and he could always throw a six by blowing into the dice box. No matter how hard I tried I could never achieve this, and I must confess that it still remains something of a mystery to me. Perhaps it was done by the same fairy who showed Daddy where the sixpence was in the Christmas pudding, and which was the longer piece of the wishbone in the chickens or the turkey. Another thing which I dearly liked to do was to

31

help him spring-clean his tool shed where everything had its appointed place and was kept shining. I was allowed to polish each piece and learned its name and for what it was used. As I always helped Daddy when he did a bit of 'carpentering' I could always find each tool as he needed it. The Trengroves had a tortoiseshell cat which was allowed to sit in the oven when the weather was cold, and the oven was only cool. Mr. Trengrove had made it a special little wooden stool covered in a piece of carpet. Of course he had to make me one just like it, so we sat together in front of the range in the kitchen, whilst he told us stories of his experiences in the goldfields. I much enjoyed these visits and when he died I missed this kind old gentleman very much. Later Mrs. Trengrove bought a lovely labrador dog, unfortunately I cannot recall his name, but we three often went for long walks together. Once a friend in California sent her a big box of apples and when we went out we had one each, and the dog waited until we had nearly finished and then had the cores. Sometimes our walk took us to an old Aunt who lived in a tiny cottage somewhere amongst the disused mine workings in Scorrier. The cottage had only two rooms, and as she was very old and wrinkled, I always thought about poor Hansel and Gretel, though of course she was nothing like the Witch. She always gave me a biscuit and she also gave one to the dog as well.

Sometimes Mother and Miss Spear, who was one of the assistants in the shop, went to Plymouth for the day, taking advantage of an excursion train. The fare was, I think, half-a-crown return. Then I was taken down to "Northcountry" where Miss Spear lived with her mother, to keep the old lady company. I enjoyed this too. She also had a marmalade cat, who had a stool just like mine, and she had two tins on the mantelpiece, one held gingerbreads and the other, peppermints. I had one of each in the morning and another in the afternoon. She entertained me by telling me about the things she did when she was a little girl. A friend of mine once told me that she had discovered why the very old and the very young get on so well together: the old tell the same story over and over again, and the young never tire of hearing it. I am sure she was right. I was always happy with older people and interested in their memories. Perhaps it is in this way that the homely part of history is carried on. Perhaps this, my story, may interest people who have no idea of what life was like in the early days of the century. I hope it may do so; anyway I have enjoyed reminding myself of my childhood, and comparing it with the daily life of the modern child.

On Friday evenings Mother and her friend, Mrs. Nicholls, who lived in Green Lane, went in to do a last bit of shopping, as the shops stayed open until 8 o'clock, and I went to spend the evening with Kathleen. Their kitchen was underneath the dining room, as the house was built on the side of a hill, and this intrigued me, as I knew no other house with so many stairs. They even had an attic which they called the 'garret', I rarely went up as far as that but when I did I thought it was very strange. Kathleen and I often made toffee — very nice toffee — made with brown sugar, vinegar, a little water and a 'nub' of butter, all boiled together on the range. Needless to say it never had time to harden, even when we put it outside the back door on the concrete, but this did not deter us from trying again the next week. I had to wait until Saturdays when Kathleen came to play with me before I got my portion. Sometimes we had 'fallen out' and Kathleen did not come, but we 'made it up' very soon which was just as well as our parents were friends of long standing.

I have always loved to dance and at a very early age I joined Miss Wolf's dancing class which was held each Saturday afternoon in the Masonic Hall in Green Lane. We learned all sorts of dancing, even once trying the rudiments of ballet. I had minute ballet shoes with hard toes and used to use the brass rail of the bed in the spare room as a bar on which to practice. I think we must have been too young for this as we soon gave it up; but I remember that when we could Waltz on our toes we thought we were 'learned out' and did not realise how little we really knew. At the end of term we gave a demonstration and those lucky pupils whose parents could afford accordian pleated frocks with frilly knickers to match stood in the front row and sometimes did 'solos'. I was never placed in this elevated position as Mother refused to waste her money on such frivolities, and I had to make do with my 'best' frock

33

usually a very nice one made of silk with smocking at the yoke and wrist. Judging by a photo I have I could dance as well as anyone and would very much like to 'show off' as they did. I attended this class until I went to the Grammar School and had too much homework to do to spare the time. But by then we had started Folk-dancing at school so I did not mind very much. As we came out of the class each Saturday afternoon our dismissal coordinated with the end of a rugby match which had been played on the ground further down the road. The hall was right opposite Dr. Willie Hitching's surgery and we saw many 'bloody' and battered young men making their way through his door, so much so, that it was a long time before I knew that Rugby was a game and not a free fight. We were all a bit frightened by these sights and hurried up Green Lane to Fore Street as fast as our legs would carry us. When I now watch a rugby game I realise how these honourable scars were received.

Before the war, German bands used to come to Britain and play in the streets of the bigger towns in the country. As we lived in Park Road which joins Albany Road to Clinton Road, I was able to hear them as they went along both these roads, and delighted to dance in the back garden to their playing. When the war came some people said that they had been spies, but I don't think they could have gathered any useful information from Redruth or Camborne. I, for one, was sorry when they had to go back home, as music for dancing was difficult to come by.

Some of my friends gave birthday parties, but these were few and far between. I do not remember ever having one myself. Christmas parties were quite another thing; there were very many each year and I seem to have been to them all. Perhaps I was invited because Daddy knew so many people. To those held in our homes not too many little girls could be invited, as the rooms in our houses were not very big; but we enjoyed them just the same. We all looked forward to them and sometimes it was not possible to fit them all into the Christmas holidays (we had only a fortnight then), so some of them spilled over onto the following Saturdays. I do not remember having to miss any, so perhaps I did not get bronchitis in the holidays, only in school time, (which I hated as I liked going to school better than most children). We looked forward to them particularly as we had such interesting food. My mother did not think much of 'boughten' cake, so made all the fancy things herself. Little sweet buns with white icing on them, and sometimes a cherry or a piece of green angelica to make a leaf, sponges with jam and cream, pieces of the special 'black' Christmas cake, or chocolate cake or coconut buns. Chocolate biscuits were a real treat as we did not have them very often. I did sometimes when I had been poorly and was 'off my appetite, but never as everyday food. There was one little girl to whom they must have been a great temptation, as she always tried to sit on a chair near where they were on the table. But Mother was wise to her, and sat her far enough away for us all to have a share. We also had pink and white blancmange with strawberry jam, and different coloured jellies in special little glasses very much like modern Champagne ones. Our custard came in little glasses too, each with a handle, just as you can sometimes see them on posters advertising Bird's Custard. They had nutmeg sprinkled on top. When I was too old to have this sort of party, Mother made jelly or custard for any little girl who came to tea, and after tea she was allowed to take the glass home with her. They were soon dispersed in this way and I have never seen them in anybody else's house.

We did not have any special entertainment at these parties but played the old familiar games, Pass the Parcel, Turn the Trencher, Stations, Postman's Knock, and Hunt the Thimble. We did not expect to get a prize if we won, as I believe children today do. One game I especially liked was one where all the girls went outside the door and were ushered in one by one to see the Daddies and big brothers each with a chair in front of him. As we came in they chanted, 'Come and sit on my pretty chair' and we had to choose. If we chose aright we got a kiss but if wrong we were hissed. I cannily played carefully and chose a Daddy whom I knew especially well and almost always got a kiss. We usually ended with 'Sir Roger de Coverley' which really wore us out and made us ready to be taken home. Here the Daddies came in extra handy, each taking the little girls who lived in his vicinity. You must remember that nobody

35

Fore Street. Redruth at the turn of the century.

had cars or any other means of transport, so it was advisable to end the party before we were all to tired to walk home, but it was fun to go with your own Daddy and decant your friends one by one at their doors and have the last little bit of walk in the dark. Sometimes I had a piggy-back if I was very tired. Some of the parents who had bigger rooms and more money had special attractions. I remember once that there was a very big cracker hanging from the ceiling with lots of bits of string hanging down to our level, and when we each pulled one a small present wrapped in coloured paper came to each of us. Very exciting to show each other what we had received. Another time it was a big snowball which we dismembered with the same interesting results. At yet another party we had very beautiful crackers by our plates, (the ones I had seen in Trounson's window and thought so beautiful and expensive that I could never have, as Mother said they were a waste of money), and wonder of wonders, in each cracker there was a

Fore Street. Redruth at the turn of the century.

sixpenny piece, put there I had no doubt by the same fairy who had thrown the dice for Mr. Trengrove and put the sixpence under my pillow when I lost a tooth. Daddy usually helped any loose tooth on its way. He let me choose a coloured piece of embroidery cotton from Mother's box, tied it round the base of the tooth and pulled the two ends tight. It did not hurt, and we usually had to find the tooth somewhere on the floor as it had whisked away as Daddy pulled. This entertainment made me forget all about the extraction, I was so anxious to find the tooth to put under my pillow. Sometimes I had to go to Mr Gee's shop to have a tooth extracted. If I was a good girl and did not cry, I was rewarded with a cachou from one of the elegantly shaped bottles on the top of the counter in the chemist's shop. There were two bottles; one held violet scented cachous and the other cachous of many shapes and colours. They were all equally slippery when put in one's mouth. One day after the tooth was safely out, and I had chosen my reward, Mr. Gee was astonished to see that I was crying. He asked my why, as that was a thing I so rarely did, and I replied sadly that I had swallowed the cachou. It had slipped down my throat before I had time to suck it. Needless to say I got another one, but I can remember the incident with great clarity.

Two or three times at Christmas 'Grandpa' Wickett gave a very big party for his grandchildren and their friends, and I was invited as I often played with Marjorie and Freda, children of his son Stanley who was a great friend of Daddy's. These were indeed "Occasions". He hired the Masonic Hall to accomodate us all, and one year a Professor Johns came down from Plymouth to entertain us. He was a magician and astounded us by producing pennies from our ears or noses, and 'hundreds' of silk squares of different colours from an 'empty' bag. We had never seen anything like it and were amazed, a wonderful appreciative audience. He even produced a rabbit, I don't remember if it was a live one, but that didn't matter. He seemed just a clever as the Fairies. Cornish people — I mean *real* Cornish people, do believe in Fairies as well as Angels.

Another year he gave a fancy dress party, and there was much discussion as to what I should wear. Mother, as always, was averse to waste money, so at last hit on the idea that I should go as a Quaker Girl, dressed like the one on the cover of the sheet music which was all the go at that time. I had a little grey dress (which I could wear all the next summer) with a wide collar and cuffs. There was a sweet little Quaker bonnet and with my fair hair (well curled) hanging down I must have looked the part as I won the first prize, much to the dismay of the better-off parents who had, some of them, hired costumes for their offspring. I was quite happy just to wear it as there was nothing to impede my movements in any of the games we played.

Once an old gentleman whom Daddy knew had to go a live in the 'Union', which is what we called the 'Workhouse'. He must have been a well educated old man as he gave me some very nice books, amongst them 'The Vicar of Wakefield', and we still have a set of Encyclopaedias which came from him. One Christmas, Daddy wanted to send him some tobacco and sweets, and as he could not go himself he asked me to go instead. So off I went, by tram to Barncoose, and the Union gate, and up the drive to the front door. Daddy had already told the Master that I was coming, so he met me and conducted me up to the ward where our old friend was. There were several old men there, some still in bed and some sitting out on easy chairs, and they all looked clean and well cared for. Some had whiskers like Grandpa and I was attracted to them. Fortunately my 'special' was one of them and he had such a kind face that I went right up to him and kissed him. He was delighted with his 'baccy' and sweets, and after I had talked to him I went round to the others and chatted to them. I expect I kissed them all as I was no respecter of persons and was very ready with my affections. Later the Master rang Daddy to say that the old dears had so much enjoyed what they called 'a little ray of sunshine' and please could I come again. I did go several times but I not remember why or how the visits stopped. Perhaps my dear old man died. I enjoyed it all very much, and when Mother threatened me with the Workhouse if I wanted to buy anything which she thought too dear, I didn't think that it would be such a bad thing after all.

I had one Grandpa and one Grandma. Grandpa was Mother's Father and when I was small, after Grandma died, he came to live with us. He was a great big strong man and I loved playing with him. My favourite game was 'Shipwrecks'; he held me in his arms and we went in a ship to Africa, or Australia, or anywhere else we thought of. The Channel was not very stormy, but when we got to the Bay of Biscay it was another story. The wind howled, and the waves were mountains high and I had to hang on like grim death not to fall overboard. It was most exhilerating. He also read to me and told me most interesting stories of the poachers he had caught and how Grandma, feeling sorry for them if they were in the 'Lock-up', (just outside the kitchen door of the Police house in Truro), used to take down the big key, cut out a dinner and take it in to them. Once when I was there I was out helping the Groom to brush Gee Gee Polly (Grandpa had a horse which he sometimes rode, and sometimes she pulled the high dogcart in which he went round his area) and I fell headfirst into one of the big heavy buckets. The Groom pulled me out and took me dripping in to Mother, saying, "Don't 'ee beat 'er, Missus, don't 'ee beat 'er. You nearly lost the dear l'l maid then".

Later Grandpa married again and went to live in Roskear with his new wife, Auntie Fanny, who was very nice. We went often on Sundays to tea with them which at first I found a bit boring, as I was allowed to read only 'The Christian Herald' when I should have much preferred 'The People', or 'The News of the World' — the outside pages of which looked most interesting, but these were forbidden. I soon found a way out of this and took one of my own books with me. We went by tramcar which was not very interesting when it rained and we had to sit inside, but when it was fine and I could sit all by myself on the little seat up in the front. That was lovely. I would pretend that I was in charge, or that I was some very important person who was to be given the best seat. I could also see all the things and places we passed. Sometimes we were extra lucky and we had to wait for a mineral tram to come out of a mine on one side of the road, go along in front of us and then go into another mine on the other side. Another thing to watch out for was the places where two trams had to pass each other and the single tramline became two, and for a moment the two trams went along passing each other. It always made me think of those horrid sums which we had to do about two trains of different lengths and different speeds passing or meeting each other!

Grandpa was fond of licorice and had in his waistcoat pocket little bits of pipe licorice, very fluffy but nevertheless much liked by me. Before we went home Daddy and Grandpa had each a glass of 'Toddy', whisky with hot water and sugar (I still have the special glass) and Mother and Auntie Fanny had port. I had lemonade with a dash of port to make it pink, so we were all satisfied. I am so glad I had such a dear old man for a grandpa and for so long. My Grandma was Daddy's Mother and lived in the cottage about which I shall tell you when I write about my holidays. To go to visit her, Daddy used to hire a pony and 'Jingle' from Mr. Gill who travelled for D.G.L. Yeast. He had two ponies of which he was very fond, and did not let anybody else but Daddy ever drive them. He knew that Daddy would not make them go too fast or overload the cart.

Daddy and Mother used to walk up Blackwater Hill, as it was long and steep, but I could ride and hold the reins and think I was driving. It was only nine miles to Allet and when we got there the pony was put into the field with Joey, Auntie Ada's pony (about whom much more later) and they had a lovely day together as they were friends. When we came home we usually had a bag of apples and perhaps cream and eggs, but it wasn't any heavier, as we always took something with us for Grandma. This time Daddy and Mother walked up Mount Ambrose and the pony had a drink in the granite trough at the top. I don't think it is there any more.

Sometimes I went to tea with Mrs. Williams, the wife of the owner of the shop where Daddy was manager. Miss Myra Williams lived with her brother and sister-in-law in Claremont House in Green Lane, and all three were very kind to me. Mrs. Williams had three sons who were much older than me, and went away to Blundell's School, and perhaps they would have liked a little girl of their own, so asked me to come to tea, and gave me some very lovely presents, a gold cross and chain when I was Confirmed and earlier two silver bracelets which I have worn ever since. The also found for me a Prayer Book and a Hymn Book, very thin they were, about an inch and a half square with silver covers. One had the "Little Cherubs" on it and the other "Christ at the Door". The print was minute but I could read it quite well. It was also they who gave me all Frances Hodgeson Burnett's books in beautiful bindings. I believe that 'The Secret Garden' was a first edition. I loved going to tea with them as Miss Myra would play with me in the garden. I usually took Lesley or Esme Joyce with me and Miss Myra crochetted for him a pair of little bootees in pink and white wool, the very ones he is still wearing. Another sister was Mrs. Tom Trounson whose pigeons we reared, and she also gave me lovely presents; a postcard album with covers of black satin which had roses and forgetmenots in penpainting on the front, and a picture of the Madonna painted on glass. This was beautiful and is very valuable I believe, as each colour has to be painted on the back of a separate piece of glass, and the whole assembled to make the picture before it can be framed. My frame was of dark green velvet. My God-daughter

41

has it now.

So you see that with all these interesting things to do and see, as well as outings to the seaside and countryside, to say nothing of holidays spent in so many different places with aunties and cousins, I led a very full life and had no time to be bored or unhappy. I often wonder if today's children get as much out of life as I did when everything was so much simpler? I don't think they do.

Outings

WHEN I began this tale of my doings as a child I did not think that I had had many outings, but since I have opened up my memory bank I find that there were more than I thought, and all of them happy ones. All were looked forward to with great hopes and many preparations.

In summer our favourite excursion was to Porthtowan, walking all the four miles, carrying our pasties, a bottle of lemonade (home-made), buckets and spades and later, bathing costumes. On the way, we left the town behind and began the journey. The road, as do all in our lovely duchy, wound up and down and roundabout. There were two valleys in each of which we stopped to have a drink from the little stream which ran there. Nobody worried about pollution, indeed we never heard of it, probably because there wasn't any. Where there was running water and we were thirsty, we drank. By the roadside, later on, there was a house with an apple tree in the garden, and the kind lady let us fill our pockets, and even our buckets, with windfalls. How nice they tasted, much sweeter than 'boughten' ones. Then came the hardest part of all, a long hill which we called 'Mile Hill', though I don't suppose it was really a mile long, it only seemed so to us. After that it was all downhill, much shorter, and at the bottom a spout of water coming out of the hedge, and collected in a half barrel. Of course we had to stop there and have another drink. Then came the enchanting place where three valleys meet, and we could shout and get an echo.

It is not strange, but quite true, that there is always a prescribed way of doing everything in the proper order, a way which must not be altered, as if it in itself were part of the doing? To alter it would bring down unknown miseries on our heads. Nothing would be quite the same again.

Then came the walk, or rather the run, over the sandy

roadway to the beach. Porthtowan was at that time a place which seemed as if it had been created especially for children's delight: a great stretch of golden sand, exactly right for digging in or castle building, or for making boats. There were endless pools to paddle or sit in, rock pools of varying depths and almost hidden corners where lurked tiny fish and little crabs and sometimes even a stray shrimp. We had shells with which to play shops, small rocks to climb, and always the sea with its waves, some tiny ripples and sometimes great breakers which one avoided if afraid, or splashed through when bigger and more venturesome. But we all respected the sea and were never fool-hardy. We had grown up with it, and knew quite well never to bathe on an ebb tide, or venture round a corner to another cove, to be cut off when the tide came in. All these foolishnesses were left to 'they queer people from up the country' of whom fortunately at that time there were very few. There were indeed never many people on the beach and we could always find our special place where we could sit, leave our clothes, (nobody stole them no matter how long one left them there), and have our picnics. We did not mind if the sand did get into the food — our mothers might — but we children were only anxious to finish it, so as to make the waiting time of an hour before we were allowed to bathe seem shorter. I had a big spade it is true, but I always hankered after a metal one such as the boys had. They could dig deeper and raise higher castles, but it was the thing for girls to have wooden ones so that is what I had. I suppose parents thought that boys were less likely to cut off their toes than girls were — why I wonder, since we borrowed them whenever we could find a kindly boy. At first, when I was very small, I did not bathe at all; I was allowed only to paddle by the side of a grown-up, holding up my petticoats to keep them dry as did our Mothers and Aunts. Only we did not call it paddling, we said 'washing our feet'. As I usually managed to get wet in spite of many warnings, Daddy arrived home one day with a pair of 'Paddling Bloomers', made of rubberised cotton in a pattern of black and white checks, and these were put on over all my clothes in the vain belief that they would keep me dry. My parents were delighted with them until I actually wore them on the beach. There I managed, by

44

accident or design, to fall into a pool, and got wet all over so they were bound to bow to the inevitable, and for a time Mother took dry clothes with her; but this was a nuisance, and there was no assurance that I could not fall in twice, so at last I was allowed to bathe. At, first, I believe, I wore and old frock with a pair of even older knickers underneath, but later I was promoted to a bathing costume. "Costume" is the right word; it was made of pink long-cloth and consisted of a sort of tunic worn over bloomers with elastic at the waist and legs. When wet it was very heavy and uncomfortable, but looked very smart and I bore with it for a long time. How I ever managed to swim in it I cannot recall, but swim I did. I don't remember ever learning, but must have progressed naturally from doggy paddle to some other method of keeping afloat, something very easy to do in salt water. Eventually I managed something between a breast stroke and a crawl, and that is the way in which I always swim. It is not elegant and does not take me very fast through the water, but I could always stay in as long as I liked, and dive through the waves and thoroughly enjoy myself anywhere no matter how deep the water might be. If we got mouthfuls of salt water we just spat it out and plunged in again. We let the receding waves pull the sand from under our feet and if a wave knocked us down we just got up and dived into the next one. At Porthtowan some young men from Redruth had built a concrete wall across the end of one of the little coves, and when the tide came in and filled it we had a lovely swimming and diving pool, deep and safe.

There were very few houses, and only one row of little cottages, in one of which we spent a never-to-be-forgotten week. Daddy came too, and we tried fishing from the beach, first digging up worms or small fish from the sand as bait. I don't remember ever catching anything, but the anticipation was enough. Whilst we were there our pussy stole a leg of lamb from one of the tents in an adjoining field, and we had to return it with apologies. On Thursday afternoons, when the shops in Redruth were shut for the half day, there was an added attraction, even though there were more people on the beach. Daddy would never come with us then as he said the beach would be full of people eating onion pasties. He did not like onions except at home, neither did I. A lady came from St. Agnes in a little pony cart to sell ice cream. She was spotless, dressed in a print frock and a white apron, and we were allowed to buy ice cream from her. A halfpenny cornet was the usual allowance, but on rare occasions I was allowed a whole penny sandwich. At the beginning of the beach there was a hut in which a funny old lady boiled water in a copper heated by wood gathered from the beach. She would fill one's teapot with hot water for a penny. Sometimes when our Mothers came with us we had tea in her hut, sitting on wooden benches at trestle tables, but we children liked picnics on the beach much better. I saw the beach earlier this year and could have cried it has changed so much. I wished I had taken the advice of Mr. Nankervis, the taxi man who had taken us round all the old familiar places a year ago, and who said, "Don't 'ee go down Porthowan Ms. Steven. You went like it; 'tis all differnt. 'Tis they people from up the country. They kent leave nawthing alone". How right he was.

Sometimes when our Mothers came they waited until the afternoon and rode in Mr. Vincent's brake. This was nice for us, as they could carry home all our clobber, and we had nothing heavy to carry on our homeward walk. The journey homewards was never as nice as the outward one, as we had nothing to look forward to, we were all tired. However the older ones helped the little ones, and there was usually a sweet or apple saved from lunch to help us on the way. Our Mothers did not have a very easy journey either, as there was only one horse to pull the brake, which by this time was heavily laden, and the road was hilly, so all the able-bodied ones had to walk up the hills. Mr. Vincent found it hard to refuse anybody, and we had a saying, 'Always room for one more, like Mr. Vincent's brake'. They took the way home through Scorrier, which though longer was not quite as hilly as the road which we took. They arrived in Redruth at the town end of Green Lane before us, but Mr. Vincent waited until we were all collected by our Mothers before he drove home himself. We lived at the other end of town, which seemed a long way at the end of such a busy day – but there were attractions to help me home: if the wind was in the right direction we could hear the stamps from

Stithians where the smelting works were, and sometimes see the flames from the chimneys. There were also electric lights all along Clinton Road and Mother made it a game to go from one light to the next, often too, Daddy would meet us and give me a piggyback.

Once, or perhaps twice, in the summer holidays we went to Falmouth. We rode there in a sort of bus drawn by two horses, and we could ride inside or outside. You can guess which I chose. We caught it in Penryn Street, at the end where Barclay's bank is now. I don't remember what was there then, as we saw the bank being built and I was intrigued as Daddy had some shares in this bank, and I wondered which stone really belonged to us. We set off along Falmouth Road, past the school which I attended, through Lanner, and then up the hill at the end of the village. Here the road became hilly all the way so all who could had to get out and walk, to save the horses. I don't know what the driver was called as we did not use his bus as often as we did that of Mr. Vincent, whose name was a by-word in the town. The journey, though not long, took a long time, but there were so many things to look out for that it never lost interest. There was a garden with two ponds in it. Ponsanooth where I used to go fishing with Daddy, and the pub where Daddy had a half pint of beer and the Innkeeper's wife came out to me with a glass of lemonade and a 'bit 'o bread and cream for the Little Maid'. When we got to the place where Redruth — Falmouth road crossed the Truro — Helston road there was a bridge over the railway, and a poor lunatic boy was always there with a fishing rod over the parapet trying to catch fish. I felt so sorry for him, but Mother said I need not be as he 'did not know anything different'. At last we climbed the hill into Penryn, up the Front Street past the market place where one pavement was much higher than the other, and down again over the little wooden bridge, now alas replaced by a very wide concrete one, and so on through Greenbank, past the ferry to Flushing and right on to 'The Moor'. Here we dismounted and after a look at the Princess Pier and the boats alongside, with a glimpse of the 'Cutty Sark' which was anchored in the bay, we walked along the main street. Such an interesting street it was, unlike any other I had ever seen, with the glimpses of the river between the shops, a very old church and an antique shop with so many interesting things in the window. It was the only antique shop I had ever seen. There was also a special shop where we went upstairs and had a really wonderful ice cream, a wafer with real cream in it as well as the ice cream. This was something very, very special, and a great treat, promised to me many times before, if I was a good girl. When we came to the end of the shops there was on one side an open space with a flag pole on it and on the other side a very old house which belongs to the Arwenack family or to the Killligrews, I did not know which, but both were names to conjure with in Cornwall.

There, as we turned to go up the hill which led to the beach, sat a lady with her little stall of kettle holders etc. all beautifully sewn, and she herself spotless in a cotton frock and a woollen shawl. Daddy always gave me a sixpence to give to her, and told me to talk a little while with her as she was there all day by herself, and probably felt lonely, as many people walked by without so much as a smile. So I always did, and gave her a sweet saved from the packet he had given me to eat on the bus, and was rewarded with a sweet smile and a few words of thanks. This was part of 'going to Falmouth' and I should have been disappointed if she had not been there. Nowadays the State would have helped to look after her, so things were not always better in the 'Good Old Days', were they? After this came a little hill, past houses where there were always lovely flowers in the gardens, and I had to stop to see if I knew their names, and then to the gates of the Gillingdune Gardens, to be visited later. Down we went to the beach! At the beginning there was a tea hut where one could hire cups and saucers, and if one wished, buy tea, milk and sugar. We were not asked to pay any deposit on the tray as in those days people did not steal the things or break them without paying for the brea-kages. Is isn't at all like that today. I wonder why? We are the same people aren't we?

The beach was very nice but not as nice as Porthtowan as there was small shingle instead of sand, so one could not make castles and wait for the incoming tide to wash them away under one's feet; but the sea was safe to bathe in, no matter

48

which way the tide was flowing. There was also a raft out to which one could swim to show off how clever one was! It was all quite safe. One would have to try very hard to drown at Falmouth. If the tide was very low we could climb out over the almost flat rocks to where a ship had floundered at one time, and on the way look for all sorts of things in the little pools left by the tide. There was green seaweed which was very slippery, and coarse bladderwrack all of which we could get at Porthtowan as well. Later in the afternoon we went up into the Gardens, where we ate our tea under the glass veranda where there was a cage of unusual birds, and looked in the greenhouses to see what was planned to be put in the flower beds after the summer plants were dead. There was also a very grand bandstand, but we were never there when there was a concert. Then came the way home. Back along the street past the corner where the lady had been, and on to the Moor where our bus awaited us. The journey homewards was just like that by which we came only in reverse, so there were just as many hills to be walked up and legs were tired and small people sleepy so that we did not look out for things which had entertained us on the outward journey. But for us there was one great compensation: on the way into Redruth we drove along Clinton Road, so we had only to get out of the bottom of Park Road and climb the little hill home.

Then there were excursions 'Up Carn Brea' – we walked, of course. Up Gilly Hill, a very rough unmade road (where Daddy let me ride in the wheel-barrow when he went to his allotment), along the top of Trewirgie Road, down Church Lane, or through the graveyard where we stopped to read the stones on the graves of people we had known and loved, like dear Dr. Edward, and that of a little girl whom we had not known, but where there were always fresh flowers, past St. Uny Church, the Rectory behind its tall trees, past the opening to Trevingey Fields where we sometimes went for a walk and crossed the railway line, (an adventure in itself), and there at the bottom of the Carn was a still-working tin mine. If the wheels on the engine house were turning we ran as fast as we could to be in time to see the miners coming up from underground with their hard hats with a candle stuck in the front of each. This was considered a bonus to the outing, and very much looked forward to. Half way up the climb there was a very smooth slippery rock known to us as the 'Sliding Rock'. We were not supposed to slide down it in case we tore our knickers, but this was one time when we did disobey, as we could not bear to miss the fun; and I'm sure our mothers must have known by the green stains on those same knickers from the bracken on which we slid. Not far away was a little well, 'Wishing Well' we were sure it was, so we just had to stop and make our wishes, quite privately of course, or they would not come true, something I think we really believed, though I expect we forgot them as quickly as we made them, for there was always something else to catch our attention.

At the top there was the Castle, at that time occupied by some people of whom our mothers did not approve, so we were not allowed to climb the tantalising rock steps to the door to buy Ginger Beer in those now-forgotten bottles with a marble in the top, bottles which have now become collectors' pieces but which to us were a bit of a nuisance, unless one had the proper gadget with which to open them. Nothing else was of the slightest use. We then made our way across the top of the Carn, passing the monument to Lord de Dunstanville, who, as Sir Francis Basset, had done so much for the cause of the Cornish tin miners. As he was an ancestor of the mine I took particular interest in this, as I have always done to any mention of this family in the history books. I am very proud of being completely Cornish on both sides of my family. Why shouldn't I be? At the other end we sat in the indentations in the rocks made by the weather, though we were sure they were made by giants, and tried to discover which were finger prints and which other parts of their anatomy. Out of our kitchen window at home we looked at the Carn from another angle, and the Castle and the monument seemed side by side, something which foxed me for a long time. I saw my first aeroplane from the top of the Carn, when we climbed to the top to see Sir Alan Cobham fly over us, a very thrilling sight! Little did I think of the many thousands of miles I should fly in later years. We used the Carn also to tell us what the weather was going to be, as it was due south west from us and that is

Henry Hawkey (author's father) with champion Linden Monogram
("Our dear Monnie")

where the rain came from. We also used to hang a piece of
seaweed outside the backdoor to tell us when it was going to be
wet. These things might seem silly, but they worked as well as
some of the weather forecasts today. So did the knowledge that
the rain always comes in with the tide. That could always send
us home from a picnic. If it clouded over when we were at the
seaside we always picked up our belongings and made tracks
for home as fast as we could.

On a Sunday afternoon we often went for a walk 'Up Carn

Marth' as it was not far from where we lived. As it was Sunday Daddy could come with us and in my early days could bring both dogs: Monnie, and Melody, who was a black and tan bitch, who also won many prizes and with whom I also had my picture taken. We went right up Park Road, past the ruined house and into a very rough road used to pull the granite down to the town for building. That for export had been taken to Portreath by the mineral line of which I tell you in my 'Education' chapter. As the quarry was disused we could bring home with us lovely pieces of gold or grey granite to use in the garden for rockeries or bed edgings. There was also, right at the top, a disused engine house with its smoke stack still standing, and we could look inside and I could imagine it working with the engine pulling the cages up from underground, such as we saw on Carn Brea. We did not go very close as it was dangerous, perhaps. Carn Marth was higher than Carn Brea, or was in a different part of the district, I do not know; but from the highest peak, on a clear day, we could see a great expanse of the west Cornish coast, from Falmouth right down to Mount's Bay and up the North coast past Portreath, Porthtowan and St. Agnes where the Beacon stood out against the sky. This reminds me of a story told about the Beacon. A local preacher in the chapel there was holding forth on the subject of "Faith", and used as a text the assurance that Faith can remove mountains. A dear old man in the congregation asked the preacher if he had that sort of Faith, to which he replied that he thought he had. Whereupon the questioner said, "See our Beacon there. Don't 'ee move 'un all away. Just shake un bit for us to see". I never heard the outcome of this, but I should like to know how the young preacher got out of that one.

Every year on Easter Saturday we went up to Gwennap Pit, a grass ampitheatre where John Wesley had preached and which has been used as a meeting place ever since. There was a large granite stone at the top and that was used as a pulpit. It is still there and still used on that special day, Whit Sunday. We used the banks of grass to roll down our new balls which we had every Easter. At other times we played with skipping ropes or hoops or bouncing our balls on the side of the house, but on

52

Easter Saturday it was a must to take the new ones to Gwennap Pit. This was one of the rituals which all the children seem to adhere to, an essential part of everyday life.

We went only rarely to another cove on the north coast called Portreath, probably as the sand was grey instead of golden because of the tin stream which ran into the sea there, and also on account of the coal boats which discarded their cargoes on the quay in the little harbour. We got all our coal from there at £1 at ton! During the war few ships risked coming so we ran short of coal, until one day one did manage to get there safely and anyone who had a horse and cart could go and fetch what he wanted. Fortunately a friend of Daddy's had such a one, a horse called Roger and a two wheeled cart, but could bring some but not a lot, as the road was steep and hilly and the cart had to make two journeys. If it was overloaded it would tip up. Apropos of this I must tell you about a time when a carter of a water cart overfilled it. The roads were very dusty in summer and it was usual for them to be sprayed to lay the dust. Water is very volatile and such a cart really should not be used for this purpose as on a hill the water will run to the rear end of the cart upsetting the balance. One day Daddy saw a poor horse trying to pull an overloaded water cart up Station Hill, which is very steep, and the weight of the water was naturally going to the rear end with the result that the horse was almost pulled up in the air. He managed to persuade the driver that it was useless to whip the poor animal, as it was quite impossible for it to move, so they let out a lot of the water until the horse could hold its feet on the ground. I expect the driver was not so much cruel as stupid. To get to Portreath we went by tram to Rounding Walls and then walked through Illogan Woods, which were always cool and pleasant, and especially beautiful in spring when the primroses were at their best. People often went there primrose-picking at Easter to decorate the churches. There were plenty for all and, of course we did not pull up the roots. Later, on the way, we passed the home of Mrs. Richards who lived in a little village called Bridge. She made me a Birthday Cake every year until I was 21 and often brought in a big biscuit tin full of the most delicious gingerbreads. She kept fowls and geese and all our pillows are filled with their

53

feathers, very soft and lovely to lie on. She did all this to thank Daddy for packing all her parcels to her husband and sons in South Africa. Very many of the people in Redruth and round about had relatives in the gold mines there, and when they wanted new clothes they sent home to Daddy. Mr. Paul, my Godmother's husband, would make the suits from the measurements which they sent and Daddy would add the pants (long), vests and shirts and send them out. He was a super packer. Nothing in the parcels ever got broken, even though all of them contained saffron cakes, Christmas puddings, and all sorts of other kinds of cakes the men specially liked. Often they would be away for years, and there were many little girls in school with me who knew their fathers only through photos. It was sad, but the women had to put up with it, as the Cornish tin mines had mostly closed. There were only a very few working and the wages paid in them were very, very low. It was a case of 'Stay at home and earn little, or go abroad and earn much more'.

When we got to Portreath, Daddy went out on the rocks beyond the harbour trying to catch fish, or at least pretending to. He never caught any, but was content to sit there in the sunshine, smoke his pipe, and I expect, dream dreams, which he could never do when working in the busy world of Trade; though I believe he did think a lot whilst planting vegetables or flowers, quiet if hard work, but then again in the open air which, as a farm boy, he must have missed in the town. I don't really know, though I knew him so very well. I would wander off by myself along the rocks, paddle in the little pools left by the tide, and do my own imaginings, happy to be there with Daddy in sight. Mother never came with us, there was nothing to interest her, and the rocks were hard to sit on, so I expect she enjoyed being by herself sometimes.

However, when we went fishing at Ponsanooth, it was quite a different story. We never came home with an empty creel, though of course the trout were not very big. Neither Daddy nor Mother liked them, but I did, so I ate them all. Grandpa didn't either. Once I took him some and he said, "Take 'em home again Cheeld. I'd rather have a pilchard." We went by bus to Ponsanooth and began by fishing down stream through

54

the fields of a farmer whom Daddy knew. I had a little rod of my own, a real proper little basket with a hole in the top through which to pop the fish when caught. When I was tired of fishing I sat by the river and read a book, or followed him keeping well back from the river bank so that no movement or shadow should disturb the fish. Casting was not easy as bushes and trees overhung the stream, and once when a friend, Mr. Williams who kept a shoe shop in Green Lane, was with us I did not manage it very well and caught 'D' by the ear." I was very sorry and cried, but Daddy took out the hook and 'D' comforted me and said he knew I couldn't help it. He was very kind, and when I was married he gave me two pairs of shoes, one an elegant court pair in patent leather and the other even more grand in black satin with diamanté-studded leather heels. I felt very distinguished wearing them and the heels lasted on several more pairs before they wore out. After we had reached The Norway Inn on the Truro road, we stopped for Daddy to have his half pint and me to have the bread and cream which the kind landlady brought out to me. I never pass this Inn without thinking of those happy days. Then we retraced our steps up river, across the bridge at Ponsanooth and through a lady's garden where there was a pond, and again by the river towards Stithians to a tiny place called 'Burras' where now there is an enormous reservoir. Until I saw it I didn't believe that our little stream could give enough water to fill it, but it does, although our little stream is now only a trickle. We used to see the schoolchildren sitting on the bridge at Ponsanooth throwing bits of their pasties down for the fish and there was one enormous one which Daddy felt he must catch. So one day he took a pasty and dropped bits into the water under the bridge, and fooled the poor fish so that he took the hook. Then Daddy felt sorry and threw him back again to enjoy more pasty meat. Nobody else ever came there fishing so I expect he lived a long time. He really was a grandfather of all the fishes in the stream. Sometimes we had to cross the stream and then Daddy, who wore what we called, 'high top boots' carried me on his back, a ride which I thoroughly enjoyed, clutching both baskets and whatever else we had brought with us. Here, too, Daddy's poacher pocket came in very handy.

Another place by the sea to which we could go when Daddy could go with us, was a cove on the North Cliffs called by us 'Skajack' but now called 'Basset Cove' as it is so near Tehidy. We went right through the yard of a farm called Carvanel, belonging to a Mr. Paul, who also knew Daddy and allowed us to use the path through his fields. Now I believe it belongs to the National Trust so anybody can go there, but there is no beach and the path down the cliff is rough and steep. When the tide was out the 'beach' consisted of a lot of rocks and pebbles but was a wonderful place to collect seaweeds, strange, exotic ones found hardly anywhere else. Daddy made a collection of them and mounted them on drawing paper. This was an arduous task as each had to be floated onto the paper, coaxed into their natural position with stamp pliers, and then dried between two pieces of blotting paper. Daddy once sent them to Aberdeen University where a professor offered to name them. He did so, but they did not all come back, so Daddy lost interest and much later I gave the collection to a Plymouth school where the science master was interested in such things. We never saw anyone else on this beach, perhaps because it was private, or perhaps because there was no sand. We took with us sticks to make a fire and with a leaf could make a kind of funnel to direct the tiny stream which flowed out of the cliff into the kettle. As this was all so different from anywhere else, we enjoyed it all the more, and it was special for me as Daddy came with us.

Sometimes we went to Tehidy whilst the Basset family were still in residence. Daddy's friend was the head gardener there and I sometimes stayed for the weekend. Daddy could fish in the lake and I could help in the greenhouse, pricking out the little seedlings of lettuce or radishes for market, as Mr. Basset was, like so many other squires, hoping to make the garden pay. Mr. Clarke and his daughter both had lovely voices, and in the evenings we sang the old church songs and hymns. Families often did this in the days before radio. We had to make our own entertainments. I remember one incident particularly, it made such an impression on me. We were going to Illogan Church and Bessie took a long time getting ready, so, though we walked very fast, we arrived just as the choir was processing in, and Mr. Clarke would not go in. He turned tail and went home, and Bessie and I went in alone. He was not cross when we got home, but he did not like to be late anywhere. Neither do I. Daddy knew many head gardeners, so we often visited them in some of the Big Houses roundabout. The gardens were lovely and I learnt a lot about horticulture.

But the very favourite outing was to Carbis Bay for the 'Teatreat'. For me this came twice a year as I went with my own Church Sunday School and also with the Wesley Chapel one, with my Godmother. We went on a special train which did not stop at St. Erth but went straight on to the Bay and that in itself was something to boast about. Once I was very naughty, and against all orders, leant out of the carriage window to see how near we were to our destination. I had my new satin purse, with a silk handle, and horror of horrors, the handle broke and down fell my purse on the railway line, and all my fortune with it. We always got extra pocket money to spend at the hut on the beach, and I had a whole shilling, sixpence from Mother and another from Grandpa. I was in tears and did not expect ever to see it again; but someone came to my rescue. Our new curate walked with me along the line, and there it lay, slightly dirty but intact, and I was able to retrieve it. It is hard to remember this as that same young man, the only son of his mother, (and she was a widow), was drowned at Porthtowan, trying to save a wretched boy from 'up the country' who should not have been in the sea at all. I don't remember whether he was saved or not. We did not care if he was drowned because we had lost a young man whom we all dearly loved. I still feel very angry with the silly people who need life-guards, yet so often disregard their warnings, and need to be rescued. We never needed them. We respected the sea and took no chances. Nor did we climb up the cliffs, which is just as well, as there were no helicopters to save us. People who lived by the sea knew all about its dangers and though thought 'dumb' by others, are not so silly after all. It is a great mistake to underestimate the knowledge of the ordinary countryman.

Carbis Bay beach was a wonderful place, with sand equal to that at Porthtowan, lacking only the pools there. We could build castles in the right sort of sand, and, much to the relief of our mothers, the sea was quite safe to bathe in, no matter what the state of the tide. After a lovely day on the beach we were quite ready for tea. This was not an ordinary picnic brought from home, but something very special which we had only on Teatreats; a whopping saffron bun, as big as a dinner plate, full of currants and lemon peel such as was never baked, except on these occasions, by Snell's bakery in Fore Street, Redruth. They were so large that I always thought that I could save a bit to take home to Daddy, whose very favourite meal was a Saffron cake; but by the time homecoming came, it was all gone 'down the red lane'! We brought our own mugs and they were filled from enormous teapots carried by willing helpers round the field where we sat in a circle. We could have had second cups if we wanted, which we usually did after those enormous buns. Our mothers had their tea in a sort of tea-room a little way away, and they had splits with cream and jam, and bread and butter as well as saffron cake; but we did not envy them. Our buns were the correct food for this special day. The buns had been brought in a large basket like a laundry basket and often there were some over, so Mother could buy one for Daddy as his part of the outing — which no fathers could attend as they were all at work on Saturdays.

When we went to Carbis Bay on other days we went by train to Hayle, walked out along the basalt ridge to the end where the ferry man would row us over the stream to the Lelant side, for a penny, and then on through the 'Nut Grove' to the bench. We never stopped at the Lelant as we knew there were 'shifting sands' there, but I believe that today this is ignored, which is silly, as all sand at the mouth of a river is unsafe.

The United Methodist Chapel has quite another sort of Teatreat. All the children walked through the street in procession, the smaller ones holding on to a rope held by the big boys so that they did not get left behind; and then they assembled in a field in Penventon Terrace and had all sorts of games and races. They too had exactly the same sort of tea. It wouldn't have been a proper teaparty with anything else. On this day all the little girls wore white frocks, (I don't remember it ever raining on either day) and each one wanted to wear a buttonhole. This was one occasion when desire outweighed good behaviour, and some gardens were raided. We had lots of roses in both the front and back gardens, and to make sure that no little girl was tempted to take the front ones, Daddy made it known that anyone who knocked on the front door and asked nicely for a rose, was taken into the garden and allowed to choose which one she would like. Then Mother or I would pin it on her frock with a safety pin (provided from the shop by Daddy) and off they all went, safe in the knowledge that they had not been naughty yet were suitably bedecked. Often the backgarden ones ran out, and we had to cut the front ones as well, and for a time our flower beds looked denuded, but Daddy said that that was what we were given the flowers for, to share with other people who were not so fortunate. He always explained to me that everything we had was given to us to share, otherwise we did not deserve to have it. He also told me never to lend money. If I could afford it I was to give it, grateful that I had enough to give. Lending often made awkward feeling between friends so it was to be avoided, but what we gave willingly we should never miss.

Once a year, on August Bank Holiday my Godmother's husband hired a 'brake' and took his family and me to Godrevy, which was too far for us to walk. We took the same road through Portreath, then climbed the steep hill on the far side of the beach where the rope railway was still in use for hauling the coal from the quay to the mines, and along the length of the North Cliffs until we came nearly to Gwithian, where we turned off over the sand hills to the cliffs above the beach. Here the sand was grey, like that at Portreath, as another tiny stream ran into the sea at Gwithian, and the sea was usually rough, but there were two or three really deep pools, deep enough for me to bathe in. If the tide was right my big 'brothers' would go in and swim with me on the shoulders of one of them. When we were out of our depth I would be transferred from one to the other, proving to me that I need not be afraid of any depth of water as it was there to buoy me up. We had to take everything we wanted with us as there was no hut. Very few people went there for picnics, but on the beach we could find beautiful mother-of-pearl shells in a soft purple colour, the like of which I have never seen anywhere else.

59

Perhaps it was the effect of the tin on the shells.

Near here was a farm called Gwelanvelan, where lived the Borlase family with whom Daddy's family had always been friends. To get there (always on a Sunday and then Daddy could come too), we took the tram to Camborne, walked along the Hayle Road as far as Kehelland, where, after going through the village, we turned off to where the ponds for washing the tin lay in the valley. There were narrow paths between these ponds and we had to go in single file along them, first Daddy, then me and last Mother. I was always spotting something which I wanted to stop and examine such as 'Mare's Tail' or 'Figwort' which grew nowhere else that I knew of, but Daddy was in a hurry to get to our destination and the only response I got to my enquiries was, "Iss come on" — so we gave him a nickname of those words which lasted a long time. He did not mind and laughed about it. At last we reached the bottom of the field right under the farmhouse, and left the stream to wander on by itself until it ran under the road just before Gwithian Church and got lost in the sand. We climbed this steep field and there we were, right outside the farmhouse, where we were always assured of a warm welcome, a drink of lovely cold milk, an enormous meal with for 'afters', junket and cream, my favourite pudding. Nowadays we cannot get the 'processed' milk to 'junk' so cannot have this delicious concoction anymore. Such a pity as it was so nice. Just another thing which we can only remember and not have, I suppose. Daddy, Mr. Borlase and I spent a lovely afternoon walking round the farm, whilst they had a very interesting 'chat' to which I listened and gathered a lot of information about things agricultural to use on my holidays to my relations' farms, (about which much later when I write about my holidays). After tea, Mr. Borlase drove us back to Camborne where we could catch the tram back home. I was tired and it was a long way from the tram terminus to Park Road, but Daddy encouraged me part of the way, and carried me the other part, and we all had a very happy day. Mother had been quite contented to sit and chat to Mrs. Borlase as they had been friends for a long time. Indeed, the Borlase family and the Hawkeys had been friends for many years, Grandma Borlase and Grandma Hawkey had been girls together and many were the tales she could tell me about those far-off days.

There was however one very sad outing, ending in tragedy. Inspector Wright of the Police Force in Redruth, who was one of Grandpa's 'boys' was a great friend of ours, and one day he hired a brake and we all went together to Praa Sands, Mother, Daddy, Mrs. Wright, Leslie and Gwennie and of course me. The journey down was a happy one, especially as I had never been so far afield before, and we were looking forward to playing on the beach. However, before we had our picnic, Inspector Wright and Leslie, seeing that the tide was right decided to have a swim. Daddy watched from the edge of the water and soon saw that his friend was in difficulties and was floating on the top of the water. He plunged in to try to reach him but could not do so. Leslie then held on to his coat and in spite of being washed off his feet several times, Daddy and Leslie between them managed to get Inspector Wright ashore, where it was evident that he was dead. Mother, Mrs. Wright, Gwennie and I had gone for a walk along the beach, but came running back when we saw what had happened. There happened to be a doctor staying in a caravan just above the beach, and he came and said that our friend had not been drowned but had suffered a heart attack. We children were sent up to play with the doctor's children who were there with their nursemaid, and all I can remember is coming home in the brake, with Daddy in his wet clothes driving and Mother and Mrs. Wright, Leslie and Gwennie in tears. It was a dreadful thing to happen but I was perhaps not old enough to realise how dreadful, as my memory is only of that drive and of seeing his body on the sand. Am I not fortunate that this is really the only sad ending to all my many outings. After this Daddy would never watch me when I was in the water, though he knew that the tragedy was not due to any foolishness on the bather's part, and could have happened at any time. I do not know what happened to the family except that the eldest daughter, Edith, married a policeman, who rose through the ranks to the the Deputy Chief Constable of Cornwall, the office to which Grandpa would next have risen had not Grandma died and left him alone. He would have had to go to live in

Bodmin which was too far away for Mother to go and look after him. In those days the highest office to which a serving policeman could reach was Deputy. The Chief Constable was always a retired Army Officer or a member of a County Family. Nowadays policemen are rewarded for good service by being appointed to the highest office in the force, that of Chief Constable, which is as it should be.

Holidays

I was a very lucky little girl in that I had Aunties who lived on farms and were always willing to have me to stay with them, so that I was half a town child and half a countrychild, having the best of both worlds. My Grandma Hawkey was Daddy's mother and lived with Auntie Ada and Uncle Matt in a cottage in Allet, in the parish of Kenwyn near Truro. She was a very thin tiny lady, and the most gentle I have ever known, although she had had a very hard life. She and my Grandpa built this cottage when they were first married. She was just eighteen and he was a couple of years older. Daddy told me that Grandma carried all the water used in building it from a little stream at the bottom of Grandma's lane. Grandpa was a cattle dealer and butcher, and there were a few small fields around the cottage where cattle could graze.

Even when I was staying there, many years later, all the drinking water had to be fetched from a little well in a field quite a long way from the cottage. To get this water Uncle Matt had made a "contraption", a big barrel on wheels, with shafts, so that Joey the pony could pull it. We had to scoop the water from the well with a jug, and then pour it into the barrel through a hole in the top, using a big funnel to direct the flow. It was a long and tiring job I can tell you; and though I liked to sit on the barrel and pour the water, I do not think that any of the 'grown-ups' enjoyed it. When Auntie Ada came to stay with us in Redruth she thought that to be able to turn on a tap and get instant water was a sort of miracle, even though the water was cold. We none of us envisaged a time when hot water also could come from a tap over the sink. The field in which the well was situated was known as 'Grandma's Moor' and right in the middle there grew a pear tree from which we could pick tiny juicy pears which seemed to have no cores. I have never seen any like it anywhere else. In the Moor too, we

Grandma Hawkey's Cottage at Allet, Nr. Truro.

could find the carniverous plant called Sundew, or perhaps Venus Fly Trap. I was very proud to take this to school to show to the Botany mistress. The cottage got its name from the well, and was called 'Springfield', and it is still occupied today; though the family who live there now have mains water and electricity, and the dairy is now a bathroom. Mrs. Cook wrote to me at Christmas to tell me that the windows have all been replaced to look exactly as they used to do, a new roof has been put on and the whole building whitewashed, so that it still looks exactly as it did in Grandma's day, and just as it did when Uncle Matt made a painting of it before he and the family moved to Goonhavern, where he then became headmaster of the local school. To me, the most wonderful thing about it is that the Passion Flower which Grandma planted to grow over the porch is still there, and flowers profusely every year, though it is well over a hundred years old. When the Cooks removed the Victorian fireplace in the sitting room, they found

64

behind it a real old open hearth, and built into one side of it there is a 'Cloam' (earthenware) oven in which Grandma had to do all her baking. First the oven had to be filled with embers from the fire, with some kindling to get the right heat; then the ashes had to be brushed out so that the bread or cake could be put in. The opening was then filled with a big stone or perhaps an iron cover. Daddy used to tell me all about this, and I thought that he was referring to Aunite Emma's kitchen, where there was still an oven of this type though it was not in use; but now I know he was describing what went on when he was a little boy in Springfield.

The pony who pulled the water-barrel as well as the gig when Auntie wanted to go to town, was called Joey, and was a real character and very much spoiled. He was very fond of anything sweet, indeed he wanted a taste of anything we had with us to nibble as we were driving along. When, therefore, we went out in the high trap, we had to be very careful, as when he heard the rattle of a piece of paper he would stop dead; if we had not been thinking about him we should have been thrown right out onto the hard road, so we always remembered to stop before indulging in a sweet or bun, get out, and give him his share, and then we could proceed without danger. Neither my aunts nor my uncles used whips. Indeed I do not remember ever seeing one in the little holder by the driver's side. But there were two little lanterns, each with a candle in it, which gave us the only light when driving in the dark. We always had to light them when on the way home from Allet at Christmas time, and very comforting they looked twinkling away by our sides.

Grandpa and Grandma had nine children, but Grandpa died before the last little baby was born, and he did not live very long. The whole family had typhoid fever and Grandpa nursed them all. Neighbours used to bring food and lay it beside the little stream at the end of the lane, whence Grandpa took it back to the cottage. This was very good of them, as in the country the nearest neighbours are many fields away. Poor Grandpa was so worn out with nursing his big family that when he in turn caught the fever, he had no stamina to fight it, and died, leaving poor little Grandma to bring up her large

65

family all by herself. In time two older sons went to America to seek their fortunes in the gold mines there, but as each was just about to return home bringing with him the money he had saved, he was killed, and the money disappeared with him. A third son went to America and carried on with the trade he had learned in Truro, outfitting, and he brought up his family there. The next son, my Uncle Willie, tried to farm the few fields, but they did not produce enough for the family; so Grandma, realising that she could not be a cattle dealer, turned to the butchering, and did all the cutting up in the little barn opposite the back door, that same barn in which I learned to milk my first cow, a very long-suffering beast she must have been to put up with my fumbling fingers. Once she had a calf and it was my delight to feed it from a bucket of milk, putting in my fingers for it to suck as if they were its mother's teats. That is a funny feeling, as though they have no teeth when so young, their tongues are very rough and give one a strange feeling as they curl them round one's fingers, but it is a very nice feeling all the same.

When I remember Grandma as I knew her, her family had all grown up and (except Auntie Ada,) left home. Grandma was so gentle that I cannot imagine her working so hard, but I know that having so many children to bring up, she had no alternative, no matter how hard or unpleasant the work was. In spite of, or perhaps because of these hardships, she remained sweet and good and very tolerant. When she heard anyone grumble, or say anything unkind about anyone else, she would say, "You never know, dear, you never know", which made the speaker feel ashamed. She herself would never judge anyone harshly. She had, too, a wonderful sense of humour, indeed of fun. Daddy was just like her. When any of the children were going to work in a field rather a long way from home, she would pack them up a bundle of food, saying, "The shelves are awful high over at Idless'" or wherever they were going. When she was very old and rather deaf she would join in our laughter saying, "I don't know exactly what you are saying, dears, but it must be funny as you are all laughing", and somebody would tell her what it was all about. Her wrinkles seemed nearly all laughter lines, but I am sure there must have been some among them caused by all her troubles, of which she had many when she was young. We all loved her very much and delighted to sit by her side and ask her to tell us all about the things she had done when she was young, and I am sure, full of mischief. Here I was particularly lucky, as another Grandma, Granny Borlase, had been her friend when they were girls, and could tell me how happy they had been and all the fun they had together. When people in Cornwall are very short we say 'they lack the inches' and although Grandma certainly lacked the inches physically she did not lack anything else. She loved to read and did so almost up to the end; although once when I asked her what she was reading at the time she told me that she was resting her eyes. She did not wear spectacles, indeed I think she probably never thought about it, and I am sure that as she grew older she had cataracts over her once beautiful brown eyes. How I wish now, that she could have had them removed as I did, and so see clearly again. Several of her children inherited her lovely eyes. Daddy did, but I missed out, I did not even get my Mother's lovely blue ones, but in most other ways I am a Hawkey and Cornish all through.

When I knew her, Grandma wore clothes exactly like those we see in pictures of Queen Victoria taken when she was old. In those days everyone went into deep mourning when a relative died and widows wore what were called 'widows weeds'. So, like the Queen, she always wore black garments made of silk or fine wool. She also wore a little cap made of fine lace, decorated with lavender ribbon and little pearls, kept immaculate by Auntie Ada. It was most intriguing to watch Auntie goffering the lace as she remade the cap after carefully washing and starching it. Daddy used to send her new lace and ribbon when it was wanted and I expect she enjoyed being so nicely dressed as she got older, as she had had to put up with coarse clothes when she was young and had to work so hard. When she came to stay with us she wore a black cape with fringes all around, and a dear little bonnet with silken strings to tie under her chin. If you cannot picture her from my description you have only to look at any picture of Queen Victoria in old age, though her expression was kind, not serious like the Queen's. I am so glad I had a 'proper' Grandma who looked the part. As she sat by the fire in a wooden armchair, such as most old people did, a chair made by skilled workmen to fit the contours of one's body, she was wrapped in a shawl, or rather several shawls. Every Christmas Mother knitted or crochetted a new one for her, and she always put it on over all the others. Auntie Ada removed one at a time to wash it, so they all kept clean. When she went to bed in the big mahogany bed in which all her children had been born, she wore a flannel nightgown which had so many extra bits sewn on in places where she said she felt the cold most especially, that it was double in some places and even treble in others. She also wore a little flannel nightcap and looked exactly as I was sure Red Ridinghood's grandma must have looked. The bed was wonderful to behold, having a red canopy over the head with silken tassels and little wooden bobbles with silken thread wound round them. To me, to see Grandma in her bed looking like a queen, was a great treat. By her bed she kept a bag of glycerin sweets in case she felt that her throat was dry in the night. I never see anything like them nowadays. They were thin circles of hard glycerin, usually lemon flavoured, and were often used by grocers etc. to stick up notices in their windows before cellotape was invented. Sometimes we managed to get her some flavoured with licorice or blackcurrent. Anyway Daddy managed to keep her supplied. Of course when we children went up to kiss her 'goodnight' we always had one. When either of us had been naughty and scolded by our mothers, we always ran to Grandma to be comforted, and often a penny was slipped into a small hand. She could not go to town to buy us presents, indeed she had very little money (no O.A.P. in those days). And when I was in Reading University she often sent me a stamp or two in her letters, and very welcome they were. There were no grants for students in those days and we had very little pocket money. Our parents found it hard to pay the very steep fees, so we expected little else.

The Post was very different then, too. The postman walked, or sometimes biked from Truro, 3½ miles, sat down and had a cup of tea and some bread and cream, whilst Grandma read her letters and answered them. Then the postman stuck a penny stamp on each, took them with him, and we got a reply the next morning. Perhaps you find that hard to believe when you realise that we have to pay seventeen new pence to ensure that a letter arrives the next day, or sometimes on the following one!

Only by having a Grandma like mine can anyone know how wonderful she was, and how much we loved and respected her. I was always delighted to go to stay with her and Auntie Ada. There were so many interesting things to do and see. As well as learning to milk the cow, there were always hens to feed and chickens to scatter crushed grain for. We never thought of maize as being suitable for human consumption, and had never heard of 'corn on the cob'. Eggs had to be collected from the many unusual places where the hens had chosen to lay them, and very clever they were at hiding them from us. They were indeed 'free range' for they wandered far and wide to keep their nests secret, though they often gave them away by clucking loudly as they came away from the nest. Sometimes it would be a day or two before we found a nest, and then there would be more than one egg in it and Auntie would say the hen was 'gone clucky' (broody) and would leave her alone to finish the clutch. Later we would see her strutting proudly round the yard surrounded by her chickens, teaching them to peck. Thank goodness there were no 'battery' hens in those days. Ours wandered around wherever they chose, picking up grit and little insects as they found them to supplement the adequate supply of grain and scraps with which they were fed daily.

The little stream at the bottom of Grandma's Lane was always a magnet to me. In spite of the fact that Mother threatened me with dire results if I got myself wet, I was often naughty and played by it. I floated sticks on it and watched them as they reappeared on the other side of the hedge. I could imagine all sorts of things as I watched them, liners in storms and floods (easy to make by stirring the water), ships bringing coal to Portreath, or taking china clay to distant ports; and most of all I liked running from one side to the other over the little stone bridge, really a miniature 'Post Bridge' as carts etc. had to go through the stream as through a ford, whilst we could go dryshod over the bridge. Another treat was to collect 'delcies', fir cones, to put in the fire in the sitting room, They look so

The author with Melody and Monogram.

entrancing when they uncurl and glow in each tiny crevice. Gorse is beautiful, too, it blazes up in an instant and the twigs make fantastic patterns before they shrivel into glowing ashes. It is so easy to see pictures in such a fire.

Down Grandma's lane grew the biggest and juiciest black-berries and in the Autumn we always spent the day there gathering them, having the lane to ourselves, as nobody outside the family ever went there. The biggest juiciest berries always seem just out of reach, even when one has Daddy's walking stick to help pull the branches down; and one is always tempted to reach just a little further. In Cornwall they grow most profusely on the hedges which were built to enclose the mine shafts many years ago, so Mother's warning was always, "Mind the shafts", to which she added "and mind the adders" as these creatures lurk in the crevices of the warm stone and it is very easy to put one's hand on one asleep in the sun. This became a family saying, no matter where either of us was going. Once we were watching Daddy coming along the lane on his way home to dinner, and Mother, looking at his farmer's gait, said, "I wish you wouldn't waddle", so ever after that was added to our 'vade mecum'! One of us would say, "Mind the shafts and mind the adders", and the other would reply "and don't waddle". I said it to Daddy as I kissed him goodnight for the last time, for when I went to light his fire in the morning I found him having a stroke from which he never recovered; and I am always glad that I did and added, "Sleep for money buy a cow", which was what Grandma had said to him when he was a little boy and what he always said to me. Such memories can be very dear.

My first stay at Springfield must have been when I was very young, as I was taken there when my other Grandma died of cancer, so I could not have been more than eighteen months old. But I went into Grandma's garden and picked off every little rose bud and carried them in to her in my pinny, saying proudly, "Ebby one Gamma, ebby one". And so it was. There was not one bud left to open, but Grandma only kissed me and thanked me for being such a loving little girl. She accepted the love behind the gift, though it must have been very hard to see her much loved garden so bereft.

It was only a small garden, but was most unusual, with tiny beds each edged with minute box bushes and in them grew all kinds of old-fashioned flowers: honesty, teazels, moss roses, gillyflowers, granny's bonnets, columbine, mignonette and night scented stock – names much prettier than their Latin ones which we hear today. At one end there was a little seat with a canopy of climbing roses, honeysuckle and periwinkles, where a little girl could sit and be any princess in any fairy tale. Then too, there was the porch outside the front door where a Passion flower plant grew right over it, a plant which is still in flower today though it must have been planted more than one hundred years ago. On the other side is a climbing rose with little scented white flowers. Daddy took numerous cuttings to try to get it to grow in our garden at home, but they never grew. His fingers must have been the very brightest green. There were bushes of lemon verbena and boy's love under the windows. It was really a fairy land to me. We picked the leaves of the verbena, dried them and put them in the chest of drawers at home to make the clothes and sheets smell nice.

Grandma died in her sleep on a Christmas Day just before her 90th birthday, but she went on living in our hearts. I can never forget her, and have tried very hard to be like her but I too often fall by the wayside.

One of the nicest things which we had to eat at Springfield was 'Thunder and Lightning' bread and cream and treacle. The cream was real Cornish cream, quite different from the Clotted Devon cream which is sold today. To make it Auntie Ada would put the milk, fresh from the cow, to stand in an enamel bowl and leave it until the next day, when she would put the enamel bowl to rest in an iron container of hot water on the side of the range and leave it until a sort of crust formed on the top of the cream. When ready, the enamel bowl was taken out of the iron bowl and put to rest on a shelf in the Dairy, where it stayed until quite cold and the crust of cream had thickened. Then I could take a sort of round shovel with holes in it, slide it gently under the cream and put the layer of cream on to a round of home-made bread. On this I used to trickle patterns of treacle, and the result was the nearest thing to ambrosia one is likely to find in this world, 'Thunder and Lightning'. Auntie Emma had a Separator, and although she used the same method as Auntie Ada, putting the separated cream in the enamel bowl, the result was the clotted cream as we know it today. I didn't bother to make Thunder and Lightning at Tregavethan as I didn't like that sort of cream very much.

My Auntie Lousia and Uncle Willie lived on the other side of the road from Springfield just across from Grandma's lane and we reached their cottage by climbing over a stile, across a field, and then over a second stile into the garden. There was, of coruse, a proper way along the road and in at a lane; but we never used it. The stile way was much shorter and more interesting. There were usually cows in the field, and being inquisitive, they naturally often walked towards one, but were nothing to be afraid of, as indeed are most farm animals. I was taught to be friendly with them all, unless they had babies, when they might think I was going to harm them and I must keep my distance. I always did this. I did not stay in their cottage very often as there I had two boy cousins and one girl, much older than I, but whilst I was at Springfield I spent many days at 'Higherside' which was the name of the farm. The pony there was called Polly, and like Joey was a friend of the family and never felt a whip. If Uncle Willie wanted to quicken her pace he would put his boot out onto the metal rim of the wheel and the noise it made was enough to make Polly 'Gee up'. There was an apple tree growing out of the hedge of the Mowey so that the apples fell onto a hayrick and did not get bruised. If there was a specially big one which we fancied, we could climb up to pick it as we, too, could land on the hay if we missed our footing. This tree was a graft of one which grew in Daddy's grandparents' orchard where the apples were supposed to be kept especially for his Grandma; so the children were not supposed even to pick up the windfalls. But Grandpa, who walked with a stick, solved that problem by pushing any windfalls out under another tree where the children could pick them up, yet not be guilty of disobeying their Grandma. I think Daddy must have been exactly like his Grandfather, as that is just what he would have done. These apples are never sour, even when tiny and early in July are ready to eat. We still have two grafts in our garden, taken from the 'Carthouse tree' by my Uncle Matt, and given to Daddy and Mother when first they came to Plymouth to live in 1932. The trees are very big now and the apples are much appreciated by all our friends.

Auntie Louisa got her drinking water from a 'proper' well with a bucket on a chain, which was let down to the bottom to lift the water up from deep down, under part of the garden. This was most exciting; first I was firmly held so that I could look down the well and see the water sparkling at the bottom, and then I was allowed to turn the handle to let out the chain until it had gone far enough. Of course I was not strong enough to pull the full bucket up, but I could hold the handle and believe I was helping, and I always had the first drink of the lovely cool water, so much nicer than anything which comes out of a tap. I expect I was the only one who enjoyed this task, which to me was a most pleasing and unusual experience. Here too there were several cows which I soon learnt to call in for milking, feeling very useful though I'm sure they would have found their own way in as soon as the gate was opened. I felt very grand going in amongst them and calling, "coop-,coop". There was usually a pig in a shed all by itself and sometimes little piglets which I always longed to pick up and cuddle like the Duchess in 'Alice', but was warned not to do so as the sow might think I wanted to hurt her baby. The sty was kept as clean as possible as Auntie said that pigs are not really dirty animals, it is only the people who don't bother to keep them clean. I'm sure that is so, as another friend of Daddy's kept one at the bottom of his garden, and she liked to be rubbed down her back with a handful of straw. She made funny grunts to show how much she liked it.

Here as in all my Auntie's homes the "privvies" were in little huts at the end of the garden, or in a field not too far from the house. Indoors when it was wet, we children had potties and the grownups had commodes. 'Elsans' had not been invented. These little houses were kept spotlessly clean. The walls were whitewashed with lime very often, and the seats were scrub-bed every wash day when there was plenty of warm soapy water. At Springfield there was only one hole in the seat which was a bit high for me, so Aunty or Mother had to accompany me, but at Aunty Louisa's there were two holes, one larger than the other, which was also lower down for use children to use. I did not find this at all unpleasant. To me it was part of 'staying in the country'; everything was so clean and smelled of 'Jey's Fluid' and there was the added enjoyment of reading the bits of news on the pieces of newspaper cut into handy squares and kept alongside. Indeed I was most honoured if I was allowed to help cut up the paper. Nowadays this form of hygiene is frowned upon, but I know that these little houses were kept far cleaner than most of the public conveniences which we are supposed to use today. Not only were they kept scrupulously clean but they were regularly emptied, though I was never able to see this done.

Yet another Auntie, Daddy's eldest sister, Emma, lived at Tregavethan Manor, only a few miles from Allet, so I could easily spend some of my holidays with her and Uncle Josiah. I was sometimes handed over from one Auntie to another when

74

we all drove to Truro on market day. At Tregavethan life went on very much the same but it was a much larger farm and there was much more for me to do. The house was older but there had been one there long ago and the date from the door of the old house had been used as the lintel of the newer one, 1666 it was, a date I had always associated with the return of King Charles the Second, as the lady who kept my first Dame School was an ardent Royalist, as were all good Cornish people, and I had early learned all about poor Charles the First and that wicked Oliver Crommwell who had (I thought, personally) chopped the King's head off. I was also incordinately proud that one of my ancestors was that very Basset who had fought so valiantly in the King's cause, and always read with pride the notice which is painted over so many church doors, a letter from Charles II thanking Cornishmen for their loyalty.

There was a big garden in front of the house and beyond it an orchard. At the side of the house there was a tiny garden up some steps, where double daffodils grew on the hedges in the Spring. It was surrounded with bushes over which I could not see, and once inside I could let my imagination run riot. I could be a queen in her private garden, or a princess surrounded by her courtiers or anything "grand" which came into my head. On one wall of the house grew a peach tree which gave fruit every year, and that was very special as I had never seen peaches in any other place and always hoped that my visit would coincide with their ripening. There was also a Victoria Plum tree which yielded yet another rarely enjoyed fruit. Tregavethan was in many ways rather special. For one thing I slept in my grown-up cousin's bed, and Irene had always been to me the prettiest and nicest young girl I had ever met. There, too, the hens strayed far and near and there were even more cows to be fetched and milked, though I never got to milking one of them, as I did not have so much time to get acquainted with either of them, as I did the gentle one at Grandma's. But best of all I liked helping Auntie to make butter. There is a great art in this. Auntie Emma had a separator so that the cream was much thicker than that at Grandma's but the method was just the same, and just as tiring. If possible we sat on the doorstep where it was cool, and Auntie began by putting the cream into a large wooden bowl, and then turning it round and round by hand. After a time I would put my hand over hers and we would stir together. When she thought the right moment had come she would remove her hand and I would go on stirring (clockwise) by myself until I was tired, when she would take over again. All this had to be done without letting the cream know anything about it, as if it did it would not 'turn'. At last there would come a moment when Auntie knew it was just right and she had only to go on until all the cream had become butter. Anyone who has made butter by hand knows what is meant by the saying, 'Coming to come, like the old woman's butter'. There is an exact moment when you feel that all is well. Sometimes we sat on the doorstep and sometimes by the stream, as in those places it was cooler, and the cream did not take so long to turn.

At Tregavethan there were several cats and kittens. Kitty Whiskers came from there, and I liked feeding them and cuddling them when they let me, but they were inclined to be a bit wild and not accustomed to being loved. Outside the back door there was a sort of yard, a remnant of the much older house which had stood on the site where the present one was built, and I think that the little cottages which stood around it must at some time have been workmen's homes, though at the time when we were there they were used as stores. Through a door in one of them a path led out to a little stream. It did not have a bridge over it as the path led to nowhere, but it seemed just as exciting to play by. I believe I sometimes tried scrubbing the stones in and around it. Anything with water drew me like a magnet. The best time of all to stay on a farm is at harvest time, and I was always glad when my holiday at Tregavethan took place just then. My special duty then was to take the 'croust' out to the workers in the field. At dinnertime a great amiable cart horse would be sent from the field to the kitchen door and I would be hoisted onto her back, one hand holding fast to the long spike on her collar and the other clutching a big basket of food and drink. There would be great pasties and thick sandwiches of pork, large saffron cakes and enamel cans of cold tea, a most refreshing drink on a hot day. Once I was safely seated, Madam would amble back to the field with me on her broad back, my short legs spread out as far as they could go, a precarious position indeed. But I never fell off of even slipped, she walked so carefully. I, of course, imagined that I was in charge, which I certainly wasn't, as she knew exactly where we had to go; but I was none the less helping, as by doing this I allowed a real harvester to get on with the work in hand, and not have to leave the field, I joined in the feast, eating with relish the sort of food which I should not have liked at home, as both the pasties and sandwiches had fat in them.

Uncle Josiah was the first farmer in the neighbourhood to purchase a 'Binder' and my other uncle liked to borrow it as it made the work so much easier. It was the fore-runner of the 'Combine Harvester' as having cut the corn, it bound it into sheaves, and threw them onto the ground from which we picked them up and stood them in stooks. I also helped to do this, but not for very long, as it was a very tiring job for a little girl to do. I do not remember seeing a whole field cut with scythes, but I have watched an expert cutting a swathe all round a field, making a way for the binder to follow. The only harvesting which I did not like was when the binder got almost to the middle of the field, and all the poor little rabbits ran terrified, trying to reach the hedge before the great knives reached them, only to be caught by the boys who wrung their necks, gutted them, and threw their insides into the hedge for other little animals or birds to eat. I once saw this and it made me feel so dreadful that ever after I managed to leave the field in time. But I must own that I liked the pie into which these poor creatures ended up. How unpredictable is man?

Another way in which I helped was when the threshing machine came, and I was allowed to stand on the rick and cut the binder twine from each sheaf for the man to push it into the machine. This was really a very dusty and uncomfortable job, as the chaff got right inside my clothes and I got a good supply of 'harvest bumps'; but felt so important that the discomfort was worth it. There was never a dull moment during the day, and in the evening just before I went to bed I was allowed to read Auntie's 'Women's Weekly', which was just as interesting then as it is today.

All these relations were on Daddy's side of the family but

Mother had some interesting ones as well. She had a cousin called Ede who farmed at Carnkye Barton, near Wendron, in the parish of Stithians. His mother, Aunt Ellen, lived with cousin Isaac and his wife and I went to stay with them as well. Aunt Ellen was a dear old lady, something like Grandma in character but was rather tall. All Mother's side of the family were tall and all Daddy's relations were tiny. I am betwixt and between; Aunt Ellen was Grandpa's sister and was, sadly, blind. On this farm there were many pussies, but all were treated as pets. One very special one, Blackie, had a shoe box by the fire, but she preferred Aunt Ellen's chair, which was just like Grandma's and like hers was in a corner by the fire. Blackie got into it whenever she saw a chance, with the result that Aunt Ellen had to feel with her hand before she sat down in case Blackie was there before her, and the puss was so determined that poor Aunt Ellen had really to push her off before she could claim her own chair. In the sitting room there was a bookcase full of books, but they were mostly too erudite for me to enjoy. But there was a special one which I was never tired of looking at. It was a copy of Bunyan's 'Pilgrim's Progress' and in it were the most horrific line drawings of all the terrors which poor Pilgrim had to endure. There was the Slough of Despond and the Giant in Doubting Castle, as well as all the tempting fellow travellers with whom poor Pilgrim had to put up, but there was also a cheering one of 'All the trumpets sounding on the Other Side', when Faithful went across to Heaven and this made a great impression on me. I had the most vivid picture of Gabriel and all his attendant Angels blowing away with gusto to greet Faithful who had endured so much. The pictures were after all very like those in the book of Grimms' Fairy Tales which we all read and enjoyed, quite as horrific as modern horror films. Children, then as now, had strange ways of enjoying the books they choose to read.

When I went to bed, however, I had quite another sort of literature. I slept in what had been my cousin Richard's room, and in his bookcase there were several bound volumes of 'The Boys' Own Paper' and I read and enjoyed all these tales of "Daring Do" and wonderful exploits. So you see my tastes were indeed catholic. Richard was at that time my 'hero' and as he

78

went to Reading University, that is where I intended to follow, and so I did many years later. Cousin Isaac used to read aloud to us, too, probably because his Mother was blind but still interested in what was going on. We all enjoyed these sessions, as he read every week the 'Jan Stewer' dialect stories which appeared in The Western Weekly News (I think). They were written in the Devon dialect which is really very different from the Cornish one, though so many people think they are exactly alike. Anyway Cousin Isaac could easily turn the story into Cornish, and many a laugh we got from listening to the strange things which happened to poor Jan Stewer. Whilst at Carnkye Farm I used on Sundays to go to the little Ebenezar Chapel on the Helston-Truro road where Cousin Isaac often preached. We walked across the field to get there and of course wore our Sunday clothes, which was considered correct in those days. After all, when one is visiting God, one should give Him the respect due to Him. The family were dedicated Wesleyans and as I began my religious life with my Wesleyan Godmother, I found the services pleasing and helpful. Once, when Cousin Isaac was to be the preacher for the day, he asked me what I would like him to preach about. At the time I was studying the history of the Kings of Israel and Judah so I asked him to talk about them; which he did so interestingly that he made it all come to life. In the house there were many texts on the walls. I remember, 'Thou God Seest Me', 'God is Love' and in each room there was a picture of John Wesley. I seem to remember that his face was stern but very kind. The very nicest picture was one of Jesus with little children around his feet and the text was, 'Suffer little children to come unto Me and forbid them not, for such is the Kingdom of Heaven'. When I had been especially naughty, according to Mother, this text gave me great comfort as I knew that He wouldn't be cross with me.

There was in the sitting room a Harmonium, the like of which is very seldom seen today. I longed to be able to play it, but my legs were not long enough to reach the pedals. However Cousin Isaac could do so, and when he did we could sing hymns. One I specially loved was 'I think when I read that sweet story of old', and am sorry that it is not in Hymns Ancient and Modern, but Daddy used to sing it to me some-

79

times so it has always been one of my favourites. Outside the yard was a big pond, but I never saw any fish in it, although there were plenty of frogs. There were also three farm cats whose job it was to catch the rats and mice, but they were also fed properly each day. At milking time they all sat as near as possible to the milking stool and were rewarded with a big bowl of the first milk taken from each cow, all warm and full of goodness. Once we missed the oldest of the family who was called 'Grandma', and though we looked far and near we were unable to find her, which worried us, but a day or so later I was playing in a sort of attic over the dairy when I noticed something moving in an old hat box. At first I was a bit afraid to go and look, in case it held a rat, but I plucked up courage and peeped in and Lo! and Behold! there lay Grandma nursing a tiny kitten. Farmers cannot keep all the kittens which appear so regularly, and she must have been afraid that this particular one would be taken away. Of course this did not happen. Grandma was given a box by the fire near Blackie's, and she had five star attention and I almost nursed the kitten to death.

Once we went to Falmouth to give me a day by the sea and for Mrs. Ede and Cousin Isaac to do some shopping. Their trap was much bigger than the one Joey pulled and had four wheels like Auntie Emma's. I always loved riding behind a pony or a cob, much more interesting than any car ride I have since enjoyed, as we went so much more slowly and the driver, knowing the countryside so well, could stop and point out to me anything of interest which we passed. Nowadays everyone is in such a hurry to get 'there', wherever it may be, that we have 'No time to stare'. Cousin Isaac's family were all grown up so I was the only child there and I enjoyed every minute. Everyone was so kind to me wherever I went to stay and I could not have been naughty, or they would not have asked me again.

Mother had a brother, Uncle Charlie, who was a butcher in St. Austell, and sometimes in the summer holidays we went to stay with him and Auntie 'Ria and my two cousins, Mollie and Freddie. He was about my age and Mollie was two years younger so we could play happily together. I enjoyed this very much until bedtime came, for then I was frightened, as the house was very old and I was sure I could hear rats running around inside the walls. I always pictured Poor Tom Kitten when he was so nearly made into a roly-poly pudding by Samuel Whiskers and Anna Maria. Sometimes it is very nice to be able to imagine all sorts of things, but there comes a time when one wishes that pictures did not intrude. I was afraid that at any moment some of Samuel's descendents would come out and bite me as I slept, so was afraid to go to sleep. Of course I had been accustomed to seeing rats on the farms but they were outside and these were inside, a very different thing. There I had been warned to keep away from 'they old rats', and did so, but here there was only lathe and plaster between us and I knew they had very sharp teeth. So my nights were disturbed and as a consequence I was often 'naughty' during the day. I did not tell Mother of my fears as she would just have told me not to be silly, as of course they couldn't get out, but I had once overheard Auntie 'Ria saying that she had met one on the stairs and that was enough for me. When Daddy came for the weekend I felt quite safe as I knew he would not let anything hurt me. In the daytime I enjoyed my visits very much as we often walked to Porthpean, along Eastbourne Road, past the 'Killing House' in the field where Auntie's servant took all the clothes to dry, as there was no garden in Fore Street, then down a lane by a wood, across the road and down the hill to the beach.

The seaside is always a happy place for any child, and I felt so sorry for those who live inland, far away from the sea, whereas we had it almost on our doorsteps. The paths on which we walked so happily are all gone, built over by housing estates; but the beach is still there and I suppose always will be, though today's children get there by car over wide roads and miss all the enjoyment of the walk. Perhaps "it is better to travel hopefully than to arrive", but it is better still to enjoy both. I am sure we enjoyed it all the more because we had to exert ourselves to get there. There always seemed to be a toddler to take in a pushchair, as one of Mollie's friends had always a new baby in the family, so Hilda had to bring the ex-baby with us, taking turns to propel the pushchair over the bumpy paths. We did not mind at all, in fact I, having no sisters or brothers, was

81

always delighted to 'mind' anyone's baby. We spent a great deal of time in the water and I think it must have been there that I began to swim, as Mollie had been taught in school and I copied her movements. Of course we had to stop to eat the food we had brought with us, and drink the ginger pop we had bought for a penny at the little house in the field above the beach; ginger beer in bottles with a marble in the neck which could be opened only with a special opener made of wood. Porthpean is a very nice safe beach, but it did not come up to Porthowan in my eyes, as the sand was not so fine and it was difficult to build sandcastles. In the summer also, Mollie came to Redruth to stay with me whilst Auntie took Fred to Hastings to see her sisters there. Poor Mollie was not a good traveller by train, so it was better for Uncle Charlie to bring her down to us. I was always pleased when she came as we slept together and played all sorts of games which I could not manage by myself. She was a very pretty little girl, and once when Mother had us both out together a lady said, "It is easy to see which is your little girl", pointing to Mollie. This did not upset me at all as I said, "Yes, she's a Basset and I'm a Hawkey".

During our visit to St. Austell there was however one black spot. We had to 'Pay a Visit' to another aunt, really a great aunt as she was Grandpa's sister, but as different from him and Aunt Ellen as chalk from cheese. She was very grand and lived in a big house called 'Eastbourne' which was passed on our way to Porthpean. Mollie and Fred called her 'Aunt out Eastbourne' but to me she was 'Aunt up St. Austell, I knew now that her name was Jane but nobody ever used it in my hearing. Around the house was a large garden with a well-raked path leading up to the front door. We were afraid to walk on this in case we made footmarks, and we were equally afraid to walk on the grass in case we scuffed it, and our mothers made things worse by constantly telling us to be careful, so the visit got off to a bad start and got steadily worse as it went on. There was a vegetable garden and also a fruit garden, but we were not allowed to pick the young peas or eat the windfalls, as I always did when out with Daddy, so there was really nothing for us to do, and Satan soon found work for our idle hands. In the corner of the garden where the path to Porthpean ran along

82

side there was a wooden seat, right underneath a hawthorn tree which grew in the hedge. Here often were people sitting to have a chat, or courting couples stopping for a cuddle. We hid ourselves in the tree, and threw hawthorn berries ('aglets' to us) down on the people, who could not understand where the pellets came from. Sometimes there was nobody there so our fun was spoiled and I do not really remember what we did until we were summoned to tea. Then began the real trial of our manners. We went up to the bathroom to wash our hands and be 'good children', and were admonished to be extra careful to get all the dirt and soap off so that we did not soil the pristine freshness of the beautiful white damask towels. Thence we descended to the drawing room where a wonderful spread awaited us, which should have made us realise that Aunt had really wanted us to enjoy ourselves; but the sight of the large table covered with a shining white cloth with the best china laid out for our special pleasure did nothing to encourage us. Though there were all sorts of nice things to eat, some of which we saw only at party times, we were too worried to enjoy them. We had been taught always to start with bread and butter, and although these pieces were cut as thin as tissue paper, one slice seemed to fill me right up. I was so nervous lest I did or said anything to which Mother might take offence, that I could manage only one small bun or a slice of cake. I was afraid to try a jelly or a helping of the very special trifle, made especially for us with no sherry in it, in case I let a bit fall and made a mark on the tablecloth. We were also intrigued by the little spirit kettle from which Aunt poured hot water into the silver teapot. We were waited on by a Maid in a black frock and a starched white cap and apron, in whom we did not recognise the pleasant girl with whom we had been chatting in the kitchen. Mollie was a gentle little girl who blossomed under these vicissitudes, but Fred and I were usually much more lively, so had to be more circumspect. Mother often held Mollie up to me as a model of what a little girl should be, which I found very trying; until Mollie told me that her Mother did the same in reverse. If Mother thought I had been very naughty, she threatened me with a "Reform School" about which she had learned when accompanying Grandpa, who had to take some unfortunate girl to such a place; but as I did not know exactly what it was, I was not greatly dismayed. Mollie was threatened with what she called "Scattled Homes", but as we were equally ignorant of what these places were, we did not let the threat worry us to much, and for my part I knew that Daddy would never send me away anywhere.

Fortunately we had to pay this visit only once during the holiday, and we must have passed muster as I do not remember any harsh words or punishments. What a blessing that our Mothers knew nothing about the 'Aglets'! Mother did not realise what a problem it had been for me to endure all this elegance, as she was very fond of this Aunt and had spent quite a lot of time with her when she was a little girl. Her cousin Annie was about the same age, and Aunt used to take them to Porthpean and let them bathe, as long as she held one end of a piece of string which was fastened to each little girl's wrist, so that she did not venture too far out. They wore their oldest nightgowns and knickers. So you see, Aunt must have been very kind after all. It was only the grandeur which upset me, I wish I had known of Aunt in those days as then I should not have been so overawed by it all. Perhaps if Mother had not told me so often to be good I should have behaved naturally and really enjoyed myself. Poor Aunt, she must have thought me a very poor little creature indeed, which I most certainly was not. She must have been sadly disappointed that we did not seem to appreciate all the trouble she had taken to give us a treat. I wish she could have met me as I really was, a usually uninhibited chatterbox.

In those days great clay wagons were pulled through St. Austell Front Street by three horses in line, and these wagons were very wide, and had big extensions out on each side so that they took up all the width of the narrow street, and people had often to go into shop doorways to allow them to pass. As they went down around the Church, the drivers had to put 'Drags' under the wheels to act as brakes; but at the bottom of the hill leading up to the Station, they would find three other horses waiting to help them up the steep hill. They all went in line ahead as the road was so narrow, and I used to wonder how each horse managed to pull his weight. When they

84

reached the top, the original three horses went to pull the wagon to Charleston where the clay would be loaded on to ships to be carried all over the world. The three extra horses would go down to the bottom of Station Hill to await the next wagon. We sometimes went to Charlestown to watch the ships in and out of the narrow harbour. It is so twisty that one would think that the ships could not turn round, but they did. I have seen them do so, and still think how clever the men were to manage it so neatly. We liked to watch the clay being loaded but it was a very dirty job, and we liked it better when our Sunday Afternoon walk took us there and all was still and dustless. Sometimes the clay was taken to Pentuan by rail, on a special little railway, and when it was Sunday School outing time the clay wagons were scrubbed out, and benches were put in them, and the children rode in style to the beach. I was never lucky enough to be in St. Austell on that special day, but I should have very much enjoyed that uncomfortable, but unusual, method of transport.

I also spent some of my holidays and several weekends at another farm near Godrevy, called Gwelanvelan, where a friend of Daddy's farmed. Here there were three little children, one a baby who was my special care and delight, as I always loved looking after any young thing, animal or human. They need very much the same care. Mr. Borlase had wanted to be a teacher, but his eyesight was not good enough for so much study, and he had to become a farmer like his brothers. but his talent for teaching was not wasted, as he took students to train, one of whom came to Reading University whilst I was there and took an agricultural degree. As I was ever as willing to learn as he was to teach, my days were filled with instruction into the ways of all things in nature. He taught me the names of all the wildflowers which abound in our lovely county, and much about the finer points of the farm animals, especially cows. Many years later when my husband and I stayed with them in Woking, where they were then living, Mr. Borlase took us to a livestock show. Whilst there he asked me to examine some cows and tell him which would win the prize, and much to my husband's surprise I chose the right one. I was delighted to find that I had remembered what he taught me, and so was he.

85

At the farm in Cornwall I learned to make butter in a very different way from that which we had used to Tregavethan. As well as the separator there was a churn which when turned did all the stirring which Antie and I had done by hand. The cream was thus turned into butter, but there was still much to be done as here much of the butter was sold. There was a sort of mangle with serrated wooden rollers to squeeze out the buttermilk. Then we moulded the weighed lumps of butter into pats using pieces of wood called Scotch Hands. For our own use we did not bother to do any more to it but what was to be sold had to be made more eyecatching, so each pat was put on a thing like a big mushroom and patted into a round shape, the top moulded like the top of the mushroom. Our trademark was carved in a pattern like a thistle, so that the people who bought it would know from which farm it came. This was a long and tedious job but I was so pleased to be able to do it that I never tired of it. I joined in all the other jobs with which I had become accustomed on my Auntie's farms. But once I had a very special duty. I was put in charge of a clutch of baby turkeys which were under a heated hatcher which had to be kept at a regular temperature which was difficult as the heat came from a paraffin lamp which was not always reliable, with the result that it had to be checked many times a day. If the heat altered the baby turkeys would die and as they were situated in a disused cottage some way from the farm house. I was kept on my toes, but how proud I was when they all survived and when Mr. Borlase came back from Henley, where he had gone to look over another farm, to find them all lively and grown much bigger. They were very difficult to feed, too, as they had no mother to show them and I had to cut up food and sprinkle it in front of them as their mothers would have done. The main ingredients which I can remember were hard boiled eggs and stinging nettle tops, but there must have been some meal as well. In this farm house there was tapped water and an indoor toilet and bathroom, all the water being pumped up from a little stream at the bottom of a very steep field by a gadget called a Flap-Jack. The stream ran over a kind of small seesaw and its constant motion acted as a pump. It was hard to understand why this tiny stream could supply so much water so far away up hill, but it did, much to the delight of all the people who needed the water. It was indeed a very simple mechanism but it never failed. I enjoyed myself there so much that I had no hesitation on going back with Mr. Borlase on Friday evenings when he had been to Redruth Market. On Sunday evening he would bring me back accompanied by his little daughter who slept with me and went to school in Camborne on Monday morning. I went with her on the tram on these occasions though on all other days I went by train. Her school was for little children and was situated in another part of Camborne from our County School.

One never-to-be-forgotten summer, Daddy hired a gipsy caravan and we spent a week perched on the cliff at Godrevy. We loved it, but Mother did not, as some pigs in the field rubbed their backs underneath it in the night and frightened her. Daddy went fishing on the rocks out by the lighthouse, and I went with him to hold on to his coat to make sure that he did not overbalance and fall in. At least that was what I thought I was doing. He caught only one very small dogfish, but we thought that was wonderful. Later when staying at Gwelan-vellan I often took the children to the beach which we all enjoyed very much. It was a lovely place to stay. One could see the sea from many of the windows in the farmhouse and there was always the Godrevy Light twinkling away just off the shore.

What lovely places I stayed in. How lucky I was. I was a very happy little girl, having the best of both worlds and never giving a thought to wondering to which I really belonged, as I was equally happy in both. All my life I have been glad that I had such a wide experience of Country Life and Town Life, and so can understand and enjoy the best of both Worlds.

EDUCATION

IN SPITE of my 'Lack of Inches' my mother never lost hope that I should become a teacher, and all my education was channelled to that end. There were several Private schools in Redruth at that time, some better than others, and some children were sent away to Boarding Schools when they outgrew the useful- ness of these establishments. I suppose the best (and certainly the most expensive) was Miss Dungey's in Clinton Road, as one of the sisters who ran it was a Graduate of either Oxford or Cambridge. I was sent to none of them, as Mother had already decided that if there were any money to be spent on my education it should be saved until later, when, if I came up to expectations, I should be able to go to a Training College or a University. I was able to read at a very early age, and learned simple Arithmetic by playing card games with Mother, Daddy and Grandpa who was living with us whilst I was very young. They liked to play Whist or Nap or something called, High, — Low. — Jack. I was dealt a hand of cards, and when it was my turn to play, I was told to play either the lowest or the highest card of the suit required, according to which was better at that time. Later I progressed to Cribbage, and as I played any number of card games by myself or with Miss Shy Nail, the simple mechanics of Arithmetic posed no difficulties to me. I suppose I learned the basics without really knowing I was doing so. My Mother had attended a 'Board School' whilst Grandpa was stationed in St. Germans, but when he was promoted to Inspector of Police in Liskeard, he decided that Mother should go to a little private school run by the two sisters of the retiring Inspector. There she told me she learned only two things, to wear gloves and to be called Miss Basset, neither of which was to prove of any great use later on. She had learnt 'Long Division' at St. Germans and never progressed any further, as the ladies themselves were unable to do so. She

Free Library with Science & Art Schools, Redruth

determined that I should not suffer the same fate, but as I was ready for some sort of schooling before I was five years old, she sent me for a little while to a small 'Dame' school in Trefusis Road, run by a widow, a Mrs. Teague, who had very high standards and was very religious. She taught us to sing several Children's Hymns, 'We are but little children weak', 'All things bright and beautiful', 'Do no sinful action' and my special favourite, 'I think when I read that sweet story of old' which is rarely heard, but remains one which I can still remember with pleasure.

Above all we learned to sew. I was barely four years old when I hemmed a teatowel, and did it so well that I was promoted to a pillow case with french seams and, of all things, buttonholes. When finished, these did not come up to the standard required by Mrs. Teague, and I was set to unpick them and do them again. This reduced me to tears, and I arrived home with a very dirty tear-stained pillow-case and red eyes. Mother, thinking as usual that I must have been naughty,

89

asked the little boy from next door, who went to school with me, what I had done. He was a very serious little boy and answered, "Well I don't know much about these things, but I think Winnie is a bit young to make buttonholes". I don't remember the outcome of this, but at any rate I was not punished. Wilfred was about a year older than I, and was very conscious of his responsibility in looking after me. On the way to school we walked along by the hedge of the Park in which there were many large pieces of uncut granite, in the interstices of which lived many fat black spiders. I was really very afraid of them, but sadistically made Wilfred tickle each web with a bit of grass to make the occupant rush out, whereupon I ran away squealing. He must have been a very kind boy, and I was very fond of him. We played together very often. His mother made him wear a pinafore to keep his clothes clean. He hated this, and whenever possible kept his hands in his trouser pockets so lifting up the offending garment and showing that he was a boy and wore real trousers.

One day Mother had us both with her in town, and as we both had long fair curls (The bane of his life and his Mother would not have them cut off) a lady said, "Oh, What lovely twins!" Before Mother could answer Wilfred said, "Oh! no, we are not related. I have not been consulted, but Winnie says we're regaged".

On our way to school we passed a large house at the corner of Park Road and Trefusis Terrace. One day when we went to school there was only half the house there. The other half had gone down a mine shaft during the night. Fortunately the family had been sleeping in the other rooms so were able to get out safely. This sort of thing often happened in Redruth, as the many shafts had never been mapped and nobody knew exactly where they were. A mineral line went past the school and we were always allowed to go to the window to watch a train go by. The lady must have realised that no one would concentrate on any lesson with such an attraction outside.

When I was five years old I was sent to Trewirgie Girls' School. At that time there were three schools under one roof, infants, girls, and boys, but each was quite independent of the others and we never met. I was taken to school each day by the teacher of standard one, as she lived in Albany Road, and passed our house, Miss Gray was very nice and I would have liked to go into her class, but my eldest God-sister taught standard two and I went immediately into her class. It was a very happy school, with a headmistress who was a rigid disciplinarian; but quite fair, kind and good, so we usually did what we were told, happily and willingly. Although the building was quite old and had none of the "frills" deemed so necessary by modern educationalists we were well taught. Of course we had no central heating. Instead we had in each room a large iron 'tortoise' stove, often dirty and belching smoke whenever the wind was in a certain quarter, (how well Miss Read describes them in her books). The lavatories were at the far end of the playground, we had no washing facilities or any other amenity. The windows were set very high up in case we ever thought of being inattentive enough to want to look out of them. We sat four to a desk, and in each desk at the top were four china inkwells in to which, when we were considered old and sensible enough to use ink instead of pencils, a favoured pupil would pour a little home-made ink (A black powder mixed with water) which did not stain as badly as 'boughten' ink would do. This was very necessary as hardly a day went by without an accident of some sort which resulted in ink-stained pinafores, hands and sometimes even faces.

I don't remember much about the lessons we learnt but, they must have been adequate, as out of fourteen scholarships allotted to our part of South West Cornwall four pupils from Trewirgie obtained places. There were no grammar schools at Newquay or Helston, so Camborne had to serve a large area. We must have learned some history and geography but all the geography I can remember was to be able to put into a map of Australia all the sheep and gold areas, perhaps because they were the only important places in those days. I envied my father, who could rattle off all the counties of England with each one's county town and river. My knowledge ended at Plymouth, which I visited once as a reward for passing the scholarship. We went by excursion train for half-a-crown and saw a pantomime, Humpty Dumpty! at the old Theatre Royal, and afterwards had tea in Goodbody's cafe, where I was very interested in seeing several children in fancy dress going upstairs to another room, little thinking how often in the future I should attend dances in that self-same room.

Of history I can remember only a list of the kings and queens of England. A most useful bit of knowledge, as later, when requested to elucidate on some happenings of a certain century or period, I had only to recite to myself this list and immediately knew exactly in what era these happenings took place. I remember we chanted our tables so that they were indelibly implanted in our memories, essential in the days when there were no mechanical helps. We also coped with pounds, shillings and pence, yards, feet and inches, as well as rods poles and perches and converted them into metric measures with little difficulty, much more easily, may I say, than we do today! In our last year before the Scholarship we learned every detail of captain Scott's ill-fated journey to the south pole, and were very glad that we had done so when we found on our exam paper the request to write a letter to a friend telling her all about it. (As if anyone would?). I did not know the date, so I asked the invigilator if she would tell me. She, sarcastic creature, asked me how I came to be there if I did not know the date. In all innocence I replied that Mother had told me to come, which was the exact truth, but she thought I was being rude. However she did tell me, and I got on with my story. Unfortunately in the afternoon when we had to do the arithmetic paper, I finished before time and asked if I might go out and look at the grounds. She said, "Look them over again". Yet again I was in hot water as I said that I had done that already three times and they were *all right*. This earned me another black look, but I *was* right. They *were* all correct. To my chagrin when I got to Camborne County School there she was, our English mistress. There was never any affinity between us, and my first year's acquaintance with analysis and parsing was anything but pleasing.

Fortunately she left rather suddenly, and in her place came the best teacher I have ever known. We were always good and attentive in her lessons. We loved and respected her, and no task was too difficult if she set it. She gave us a love and knowledge of our language and literature which I have never

The Author, Trewirgie Schooldays.

lost, and for which I am ever grateful. Sadly, during my last term at school, she contracted multiple sclerosis and had to leave. I kept in touch with her until she died. Much of my future career depended on the foundations which she had laid so securely in my mind.

But to return to Trewirgie. The bane of my life there was

93

'sewing', probably because of my first unhappy acquaintainship with that pillow-case. However here it was entirely different, and to my mind much worse. At first we were given a small piece of calico to hem. We had to use red cotton so that if our stitches were uneven they had to be picked out and done again. Having survived this initiation we had two pieces of the same sort of calico and had to join them together with a 'run and fell' seam and after that a 'seam and fell'. By this time the calico was dirty and bloodstained from pricked fingers. My adventures with the pillow-case helped me to accomplish these tortures with little trouble, but more was to come. We were given two short steel knitting needles and initiated into the mysteries of plain and purl. Here again I found doing the actual stitches easy, as I had already knitted mother a tea-cosy in pink and green 'double berlin' wool; but I found these little needles hard to handle after the large wooden ones I was accustomed to, and one day I ran one of them into my thumb, which not un-naturally turned septic, and took a long time to heal, in spite of Mother's hot poultices; and even today, when it is very cold, I have to clench my fist with that thumb inside to keep it warm. We still had not plumbed the depths of misery. We had to learn to use four of these instruments of torture and knit stockings, turn each heel and graft each toe.

When we had conquered all this we were let off knitting and progressed to a further form of sewing before which all our former totures seemed as nothing. The first garment chosen by our betters for us to make was a pair of knickers. First of all we joined each leg separately, why I don't know, as the result was that almost every little sufferer made both halves for the same leg, so that we each had either two right legs or two left ones. Sometimes it was suggested that a way out of this difficulty was to swop one of our legs with a correct one sewn by someone else. This was agreed to by those whose sewing was not up to scratch, but frowned upon by those who had managed to do nice even stitches. I was definitely not going to do this. For one thing my legs were still clean, and for another my calico was finer than any one else's as Daddy brought it home from shop and had chosen the best there. So I had to pick mine out and do it all again, by which time it was as grubby as

94

all the rest. I still can't see why we could not have sewn up the front and then the back, and finally all round inside the legs. But we didn't, and "ours not to reason why". But then came the worst part, the bottom of each leg had to be gathered into a band and a frill or lace attached to the bottom of this band. If you had a clever mother she crochetted the lace for this part, mine did, but it was much harder to fit into the band. Then the side of each leg was cut down and the raw edges hemmed. But were we finished? Not on your life. The fronts and backs were also inserted into bands and each adorned with buttonholes to attach them to our 'Stays'. Then came 'the unkindest cut of all', a gusset, to be inserted at the bottom of each hemmed side opening. A gusset is a triangular piece of cloth which has to be folded in a special way and put in so as to strengthen the opening. I won't try to explain how it was done, I don't think I could, but I could still insert one if I had to. All men's shirts had to have them so every wife who made her husband's shirts had to know how to do it. Fortunately Daddy bought his shirts ready-made so we did not have to bother ourselves with such things, thank goodness, and nowadays no such things are in use, everything is done by machine and handwork, such as we learned, is rarely used.

If we showed any aptitude at these devilries we were again promoted, this time to pinafores, Sunday best ones of white Madapolam or fine linen. Here we learned how to pull gathers up as tight as possible so as to 'stroke' each gather by itself, then pulled out again to fit the front yoke of the pinny and hemmed in, with one stitch to each gather. After this came more frills, lace or even tucks in various parts of the garment, and when finished it was either a work of art or a mess. Those of us who got over all the hurdles wore our pinafores with pride and took good care we did not get them dirty, as washing and ironing all those gathers and frills would have been beyond us.

Many years later, when I was asked to go to Admiralty House to judge the work of the 'Naval Wives' Club', there was one old lady who had been taught just as I had been, and her work so far surpassed anything the others entered that I had to give her the cup. After this happened two years running I asked the officer's wife who ran the club, if I could donate a prize for the best work presented by anyone who had never received anything. This request was granted and I was very happy, as if I had had to give the cup to this same old lady every year there would soon have been no entries. Some very good sewing and knitting was done the results were given to the Royal Naval Orphanage. Unfortunately the harbour master's wife who ran it, had to leave as her husband was promoted, and no body else wanted to take it on, so it folded up; such a pity as all the women were so friendly and enjoyed their afternoons together.

While I was at Trewirgie various festivals were held in Redruth and Camborne and Miss Harris, the headmistress decided that it would be nice for her school to send in a choir, as we had a very good music teacher. As I was unable to keep in any key for more than a few bars I was not included. I was very disappointed as I liked to be in everything and had a non-singing part in a Cantata which we presented in the Druids' Hall. Miss Harris, feeling sorry for me, said that I could join the choir as long as I did not sing, only mouthed the words. Honour was served, but for some reason or other the festival did not take place, and we were all upset about it, I as much as those more talented girls who had spent so long practising.

In September 1913 I left Trewirgie and took up my scholarship at Camborne County School. This scholarship had loomed up throughout my life in Trewirgie. There were only so few to be obtained, and if one did not pass one's parents had to pay for one to attend the county school and so pass on to higher education. If one was successful, tuition and books were free, though in the higher forms it was helpful if one could have for one's own many more books to enlarge one's knowledge of the more advanced study of the English language. We worked at first for a junior examination set by the University of Cambridge. This was usually taken at the age of 15 but as I was so much younger than most of my class mates I managed it at 14. The subjects required were arithmetic, algebra, geometry, a language (French in our case) history, geography, scripture (old and new testaments) English (language, syntax and

96

Author at end of the Great war, just before going to Reading University.

literature) art and a science (botany for us). All these had to be presented in the examination, there was no choice. Two years later we took the same subjects in the Senior Cambridge and to pass it was necessary to do well in all except art, thank goodness. I managed to get "good" in each part of each subject so was exempted from retaking the exam to achieve matriculation which was necessary for entrance to a university. As two other subjects, trigonometry and Latin, were also necessary and they were not included in the school curriculum, I studied these on my own, and managed to get the required standard in both so was accepted for Reading and went there very happily at the advanced age of 17½ years.

When I first went to Camborne I decided that I must work extra hard to be top of the class in at least some of the subjects as I had my eye on the lovely prize books which were to be earned in this way. My God-sister had several in her bookcase, beautiful red books, bound in leather with the school badge on the front. So I worked my very best, and not only did I get top in three or four subjects, but I was top of the whole class. I dreamed of the Prize-Giving day and had already chosen what titles I would chose. Then came the shock. The War had broken out and the managers had decided that the money usually spent on the prizes should instead be given to the poor Belgians. I was completely overcome. I could not see why my efforts should go unrewarded. It clouded all my school life. I am ashamed to say it, but I hated those poor creatures and the managers even more, and to this day I do not believe that Belgians got the money. I am sure they never benefitted by my unwanted sacrifice. I decided then and there to work even harder to spite them. I am sorry I was so mean-spirited but I was, after all, only a little girl and it seemed to me as if my whole-hearted efforts had led to nothing. I had already seen those lovely books in my book-case, and now for ever I should have nothing to show for all my hard work. When presented with a piece of paper, such as was given to nearly everyone in the class, I tore it up and threw it on the floor. Of course I was punished for my ill temper and even more for being so impolite but I did not mind. I had shown them all what I thought of them. Daddy said I should not have been rude as he did not think his little girl would be impolite, and that was a much bigger punishment than any of the others, which I must say I have quite forgotten; but he did add that he knew how much I had wanted those books and how hard I had worked; but added that I had learned that one did not always get what one wanted or deserved in life.

In spite of this I enjoyed my years at the county school. I found the lessons interesting and that I could easily get good marks if I worked hard enough. It was not that I wanted to 'beat' any of my friends, only that I had set myself a goal and would not be turned aside. So I remained top of each class as we worked up through the school, but still remained good friends with my classmates who did not manage to get such high marks. Indeed I have since been told by some of them that they did not dislike me for doing so, as I was always ready to help anyone who asked me.

All during my childhood and early youth I found it difficult to see what was written on the blackboard, and stayed behind at playtime to copy it before it was cleaned off. Also much later, when we had a cinema in Redruth, and I was taken to see the silent films, I had to ask Mother what was written underneath the action, only to be told to read it for myself. I did not have a wrist watch, when most of my friends did, as Mother said I could not have one until I could tell the time, which I found impossible from a wall clock; as what I thought I saw was often quite wrong. Daddy very much wanted me to learn to play the piano, and I tried very hard, but seemed always to play the wrong notes. I could do the theory quite easily, but the actual playing always eluded me. We did not have our sight tested in school, so I had no idea that I was different from anybody else. I accepted Mother's decision that I was being a nuisance, but did not know why. When given any problem for homework, I could get it right if it was set from a book, but if it had been written on the board I often could not understand why it seemed impossible, When I was utterly lost, I used to go up to Winnie Martin, who was the daughter of Mother's best friend, and who, being two or three years older than I, could tell me where I went wrong, almost always in the copy I had made. In spite of this nobody seemed to realise why I got into such difficulties until I had to have my eyes tested before I went to Reading University. There being no oculist in Redruth I went to a dear old man in Truro, who after testing me, said to Mother. "I don't know how this poor child has ever learnt anything in her life. She can't see much beyond her nose". Mother was most annoyed and said, "I don't know why she should be short sighted; Nobody in my family is". However the oculist gave me Pince-Nez glasses to wear when I had to use them in lectures, but said that, as I had managed without them for so many years, I might as well continue to do so, which I did for a long time. When I put them on for the first time at home I said, "Why, you can see the leaves on those trees." I knew they had them, but I have never seen them before". Then I was allowed to have a wrist watch and Daddy was very distressed that he had not noticed my disability before.

Another thing which I began in Camborne school was folk dancing and that I have enjoyed all my life and still do. We had a gym teacher who had been trained at Chelsea, and there had come under the influence of Cecil Sharp, and her enthusiasm made us all devotees. We even won a shield at the first festival held in Cornwall, and very proud of it we were. We gave demonstrations at several functions, and as we had to wear our school uniform, I thought it ought to be livened up a bit; so Daddy gave me yards and yards of wide black hair-ribbon, and an equal length of narrow gold, and I spent hours sewing the gold down the middle of the black so that we could all have beautiful big bows in our school colours on our pig-tails. We felt very grand, I can tell you.

Food

We had plain food but plenty of it, though neither of us had a big appetite. Mother was a good cook and, like all Cornish people, she made a batch of Saffron cake and buns every week. Daddy was very fond of it and always finished his dinner with a bun or a slice of cake and a cup of tea no matter what we had had for the main meal. Mother did not make her own bread very often but my Godmother, Mrs. Paul did; a great batch every week, and it was my delight to watch her doing it and to have a little loaf all for myself when she had finished. Mother also made sweet cakes or small buns with currants or sultanas in them. These were baked in 'Patty Tins' as were meat patties and mince pies at Christmas. We often had jam tarts with which we had cream. She was a good hand with sponges too. They always rose beautifully and tasted very nice with two sponges put together with jam or, on special occasions 'butter cream'. Before the War we had never heard of margarine, indeed it was a long time before Mother could be induced to use it. Butter was used for cakes and 'butcher's' lard for pastry. I don't remember 'self-raising flour' I think plain flour was used for pastry and a little baking powder added for buns, cakes and scones. In the Spring when the cows had 'come in' (had had their calves) there was a surplus of milk, so farmers' wives made an extra lot of butter. We used to go to a small farm near the Old Reservoir and buy as much as the lady could spare, as it was much cheaper at that time as well as plentiful. When we got home Mother 'salted it down' in a 'buzza' an earthenware jar very much like the ones in which the 'forty thieves' hid, though much smaller. She put a layer of butter then a layer of salt, and so on until the jar was full. We used to buy our salt either in big oblong lumps from the grocer or, in even larger lumps cut off an enormous one from an old man who called at the door. It was my job to cut up the salt, roll it with a rolling

101

pin and put it in a special earthenware salt jar. I still have the one we used. When later she wanted to do some cooking she would take out a piece of butter wash out the salt by squeezing it out under the tap and, use the by now salt-free fat to make the cakes or buns. As I have said, she used lard for making the pastry for pasties, which we all liked very much. What Cornishman doesn't? The contents were usually best steak (which I cannot now afford) potato and turnip for Daddy and me, with onion for herself. We two did not like onion in our pasties, but Mother remarked that if a bit of hers was left we could always eat it up for tea! She also made apple pasties, jam pasties and often 'Figgy' (Raisin) ones. Cornish people seem able to put almost anything in a pasty. Indeed it is said that the Devil will never come to Cornwall because he is afraid he will be put in a pasty!

Also in Spring the hens 'come to lay' and eggs were reasonably cheap; so Mother bought a lot and 'put them down' in Ising-glass in a special pail with another wire pail inside it so that the eggs could be easily taken out when wanted for baking. They were no use for frying or boiling but most useful for cakes and buns. We often had fish, hake, whiting or pollack which she bought from a shop at the top of the town, but more often from an old fisherman from Porthleven who drove up in a pony trap and started at the end of Clinton Road shouting, "Pilchards, Pilchards, two a penny aich!" He was called Jory, and had such a loud voice that we could hear him coming, and Mother sent me down the hill with a big plate to buy some. When they were very plentiful she went herself with a 'frail' a woven straw bag, and bought a lot which she salted down in yet another Buzza to be kept until fish became dear in the winter. We had them boiled or best of all, 'scrowled', put between two parts of a sort of wire grill and pushed right into the fire. This made the range very greasy but they tasted delicious, and even the bones could be eaten as they were all 'grizzled' up. Perhaps people learned this way of cooking from the Gypsies who often came to our door to tell fortunes and beg, or try to sell clothes pegs, which they had made from twigs taken out of the hedgerows. We bought them as they were the only pegs we saw. I don't remember the ones we now

102

use with wire springs in them. Pilchards are very hard to clean as they have so many thickish scales, and it was often my job to wash them off under the tap, which I quite liked doing in the summer when the tap water was fairly warm, but hated in the winter, as you can guess. They were very cheap and nourishing and were eaten in great quantities by people living near the sea who could be sure of getting them fresh from the sea. They came along the coast in great shoals and a man used to stand on a cliff-top and watch for them. When he saw the colour and movement of the sea change he recognised what was happening and shouted, 'Heva', and all the fishermen went out in their boats to catch them. There was no such nonsense as a "quota" then and we didn't have 'foreign' boats coming from France or Russia or even Scotland to steal our fish as the poor fishermen have nowadays under 'Common Market' laws.

Sometimes Mother would 'Marinate' the fish, putting them in a deep dish with vinegar and spices and a bay leaf for flavour. When she did this I was sent down to Mrs. Paul to get a bay leaf, as she had a tree in her garden. Needless to say I did not need a second bidding as I always loved to go there, my second home.

On Sundays we always had a roast dinner, pork, or lamb or Sirloin, which is now almost too dear to buy except at Christmas, for a treat. We also had stews and pies and 'under-roast' which is made like a pie but with sliced potato on top instead of pastry. I remember that when Mother made a pie she bought best steak, cut it in smallish thin slices, put a little bit of fat inside each piece, rolled it in seasoned flour and laid each piece carefully in the pie-dish with a little water before she put on the pastry lid. Sometimes we went down to Plain-an-Gwarry at the other end of the town to a little shop which was a sort of off-shoot of the Redruth Bacon Factory, where we could buy what we called 'roll of pork' which is I believe sold today as 'tenderloin' and can be used in 'Viener Schnitchel' instead of veal. She rolled this up with stuffing in the middle and roasted it, or sometimes made pork pasties or patties with it. Either way I liked it very much as there was no fat, and fat made me sick. When she also bought a cow's heel and pig's trotter she made brawn with hardboiled eggs in it, and it set so firm that it could be cut in slices and put into sandwiches for me to take to school for dinner, which I had to take with me when I went to Camborne County School, as there was not enough time at mid-day to come home to Redruth and go back again. Sometimes the butcher would put a piece of brisket in his brine and when Mother had boiled it she put it in a round cake tin with a 'goose' on top to press it. A 'Goose' is a very heavy iron which is used in tailoring to press men's suits etc. We had one of which the handle had broken off, and it, as well as being heavy, fitted exactly into the cake tin. With this boiled beef we usually had a suet pudding, and if there was any left over we put treacle on it and called it 'Pudden out for Treacle' which is what Daddy had called it when Grandma had made it for her family when he was a little boy. Mother also had an ox tongue put in the brine and after boiling it she waited until it was cool, skinned it, rolled it up, and put it in the cake tin just as she had done with the beef. Both of these foods tasted very much better than the cooked meats which we buy today. There was a tripe shop at the top of the town, and here Mother bought tripe. She liked the thick part, and never bought 'Bible' which was lots of thin pieces like the pages of a book. The lady in the tripe shop was very kind and I often saw her give a big piece to an old woman for a penny. I liked tripe stewed or fried or just as it was. Grandpa liked it best like this. Also there was no fat. That pleased me. For puddings we sometimes had suet pudding with 'figs' in it, 'figgy duff', and also all kinds of milk puddings. Daddy's favourite was egg custard so we had that very often. To stop the milk from curdling Mother put the pie-dish into another which had water in it, so using a 'Bain Marie' though of course she had never heard of such a thing. At the right seasons of the year we had fruit tarts or stewed fruit with custard, or cream which I fetched from a dairy in the back garden of a lady who lived in Albany Road, just above us. She would first weigh my cream glass and then put in the cream and weigh it again. She was a good hand at guessing the weight, which was always a quarter pound, and I believe I paid sixpence for it. It was of course real Cornish Cream, not so thick as the clotted cream sold today, but with a much nicer flavour. We had sponge puddings with jam or mincemeat which I had helped Mother to make at Christmas time. This entailed a lot of work as the suet was bought from the butcher and had to have the skinny bits removed and the pieces which were left chopped up very fine. Then there were the lemon and orange peels to be sliced after I had removed the sugar in the middle of each half fruit. This was a nice task as I was allowed to eat the sugar which tasted of the fruit which had been candied in it. It was not so pleasant to take the pips out of 'figs' or the skins off the almonds, as my fingers got very 'Washerwomany' but I was allowed to eat some of these so it had its good points. I think there were other fruits in it as well but I cannot remember having to prepare them. Much the same things had to be done when Mother made her Christmas cake. Every lady made one of these every Christmas. It was called a 'black cake' because it was dark in colour, and was a very special one. Some people put icing on their cake but most mothers put a thick layer of almond paste and stuck blanched almonds in that. After both of these cooking efforts there was a bowl to lick out, very tasty, so I liked this time of year very much. Christmas puddings were made of very similar ingredients but they had to be boiled for hours in an oval saucepan used only at Christmas, and then again for an hour or so on Christmas Day. I never saw any threepenny bits put in these puddings, but Daddy always gave me a piece in which I could find one. Fairies again, you see.

We drank tea, not coffee. The only coffee I remember is Camp Coffee which came in square shaped bottles with the picture of a Highland soldier on the label. Somehow it was printed so that this picture appeared again and again as if in a mirror, very puzzling.

Once inside the cardboard packet I found a paper serviette with the same picture on it. It was the very first paper serviette I had ever seen, and it made a very nice tablecloth for my dolls' teaparty for a long time. Very few things were sold in closed packets as they are today. Sugar was scooped out of a sack and when weighed, sold in blue paper bags, whilst currants etc. usually had green paper. Custard powder sometimes came in 'Pooks' just like the ones we had our sweets in. Most things were bought in bulk by the grocers and weighed out as wanted. Mother always bought 8¾ 1b flour. She was very fussy and washed all the fruit for cakes etc. very carefully before using it. I am sure that this was necessary as I remember finding little pebbles and stalks in the fruit which I was given to wash. That was why she would never buy 'Boughten' cake (except at Tea-treat time) and if we ever went anywhere to have tea in a cafe, she would not go into one until she had looked round the back, to see if the tea towels hanging on the line were nice and clean.

This sometimes took up a lot of our time in a new town but she was adamant. At Christmas, too, everyone made a very special rich saffron cake and each mother had her own special recipe. We all gave our friends a bun to taste. Some were naturally better than others, but it was hard to choose between them. At this time even Daddy had enough saffron cake, as each of his young ladies brought him one to try and as he employed over thirty girls there were very many to taste. Of course he never found any one better than any other, but he always said that Mrs. Stanley Wickett made the best cake of all. Mother did not seem to mind.

We also had biscuits, and could see to choose which ones we wanted as they were displayed in tins with glass in the lids, and stood in front of the counter in the grocers' shops. I do not remember any being wrapped, except Cream Crackers. If some of the biscuits got broken we could buy them cheaply. Nowadays before we have managed to open the packets we have broken some ourselves but they are no longer cheap. Some of our favourites have disappeared altogether like my breakfast biscuits and puff cracknels, and the ones which are left, taste as if they are made with flour, water and no flavouring, whereas in those days one could taste the butter in them. We had fruits in their season and nuts and oranges only at Christmas. Of course we had none of the exotic fruits we see in the market today. Sometimes Daddy bought me a pomegranate, but they were so hard to eat, picking each little bit with a pin and then spitting out the tiny stone in the middle, that I did not really enjoy them, but had to have one all the same. We called Brazil nuts 'pasty nuts' and liked them very much, but rarely man-

106

aged to get a whole one out when we cracked it. Walnuts were the same, very mangled after we had done with them, though I do remember one year that we used a knife to cut them in half and made dolls' House furniture from them, as we did with chestnuts, pins and coloured cotton. Chestnuts could be roasted by the open fire on the grating, and were delicious, though we sometimes burnt our fingers and even our mouth's as we could not wait for them to cool. In our Christmas stockings we had a new penny, some nuts, an apple and an orange, and the rest was filled with some treasures which our parents had been saving up for us. I would have liked to have one of those 'made-up' stockings which I saw in the shops, but Mother would have none of them, 'waste of money', said she, and was probably right. She was a good economist, otherwise I should never have been able to go to a University. There were no grants in those days.

On Christmas Day Daddy hired Mr. Gill's pony and we went to Allet to spend the day with the family and we had goose for dinner with Christmas pudding and mince pies to follow. Grandma always made a 'chop potato pudding' to cook under the goose and it was lovely. In fact I think Daddy liked it best of all. When any was left we had it fried the next day. The giblets were made into soup and I especially like sucking the meat of the webbed feet. With the fat which was left from roasting the goose Mother made a very special kind of dough bun for Daddy, with salt instead of sugar and caraway seeds instead of fruit. When I was poorly and had even less appetite than usual Mother made me 'beef tea' by cutting up shin of beef into very small pieces, putting them in an earthenware jar, covering them with water and putting this into the oven and leaving it there for a long time until all the goodness had come out of the beef, and what was left was very nourishing soup. It tasted very nice, and Mother gave it to me to 'slock' my appetite. When we had eaten some of the Sunday joint there was usually left on the dish some sort of jelly, which I called 'red gravy', and I could have it for supper made into a soup with hot water, and with it some small pieces of bread. Grandpa liked 'kidley broth' bread soaked in hot water with butter, salt and pepper added. It doesn't sound very nice, but I like it and often had it for supper, especially when Grandpa lived with us, as I always wanted to have what he had. We also had stew, both kinds, thick and thin. The former sort, as well as meat and vegetables was thickened with lentils and pearly barley, but the latter had only meat and vegetables. The meat used was always 'shin' as it goes to pieces when boiled slowly and makes lovely gravy. Do you know that Cornish people say, "Gone Abroad" when potatoes or any fruit or vegetable goes really soft when cooked? We had plenty of fresh vegetables as Daddy grew them in his allotment. I am sure our food tasted better and was more nourishing than the 'convenience' food which we can buy today. Neither we nor the butchers had refrigerators; but I do not remember anything 'going off'. Apples, peas and beans were often sold at the door by men who measured them in gallons, not weighed in pounds. Milk was delivered to our door by a dear old man whom we called 'Mr. Kerjig' but what his real name was I never discovered, probably some very Cornish one like Trewavas or Kerjarrick. He brought the milk in big churns and measured it out into cans which he emptied into our jugs. One morning he came without his cart, and told Mother that he would not be able to bring us our milk for several weeks as his little niece, who lived with him, had scarlet fever. Happily she recovered and he returned, but I don't remember from whom we bought our milk in the meantime, nor do I know what became of all his milk. Cows do not stop just when they are told to do so, as the Common Market people seem to think they do. Perhaps the little calves got it instead. I hoped so, as I often wondered why I had to feed them from a bucket, holding my fingers in the milk as if they were the cow's udders. It was a funny feeling as their little tongues are so rough. I liked doing it though. On Boxing Day Mother's brother and his wife and two children came down from St. Austell and we all went out to Roskear, to Grandpa's. His second wife had kept a hotel in Newquay, and for dinner we had turkey with all the trimmings, brandy sauce as well as cranberry sauce. Grandpa carved the bird, and afterwards when we had the Christmas pudding we three children always got a threepenny piece each, as we had done at Allet. There you see, Fairies again! No wonder I believed in them, sixpences in crackers, to say nothing of the pennies Daddy found in the back lane when I walked down it with him, on my way to school! Daddy, or Grandpa, or any of my uncles always carved the joint, and served the pudding; and when later I saw a mother doing it I thought it very strange.

We had plenty of varied meals and menus, though our mothers had never heard of 'balanced diets' or carbohydrates or vitamins etc. or any of the strange additives printed on all the packets today. Bread was made of flour, white or brown, whichever one wanted, yeast and salt, with perhaps a little butter. With the milk we could make junket with rennet, to eat with cream. Now the milk has been so messed about that it won't 'Junk' and that is one delicious thing which we can't have. Jam was made at home with fresh fruit, and marmalade with Seville oranges when they were in season. Of course there were many 'boughten' things but most people made everything themselves which was much cheaper and tastier. Our mothers did not seem to mind the extra work, and there must have been plenty of it.

I forgot to say that at Grandpa's we had, 'muscatels and almonds' which seemed to me to be the height of luxury as I never saw them anywhere else, except in Trounson's Grocery shop in a sort of triangular packet with pictures of grapes and leaves on it. I did not realise that they were really the same 'figs' which I had had to de-pip and the same almonds as those from which I had taken off their skins. So easily are the public, (not only the young ones), attracted to fancy packings, something which cosmetic manufacturers realise even more than other manufacturers. Today we are overwhelmed with packets on everything and all of them are so difficult to unwrap that sometimes we wish we had not bought them. Without them there would not be so much mess on our pavements as so many people unwrap something they want to eat or smoke, and, just discard the wrapping wherever they happen to be at the time. A sign of the times, I suppose.

The War

I SEEM to have said little about the "Great War" which was supposed to end wars, probably because it did little to alter my life. After all, I was only twelve years old when it broke out, and the following years were spent in working very hard in school, or enjoying myself on various farms during the holidays. The only relative of 'Calling-up' age was a cousin who had emigrated to Australia, joined the Army there, was sent to Gallipoli, was wounded, and came back to Britain and did not have to go away again. All my uncles were too old and my cousins too young. My Godmother's three sons where "somewhere in France" but I did not realise how great the danger was. We made them toffee out of saved-up sugar, but it was very sticky and I always wondered how it got to them. They all came back safe and sound, for which we thanked God, but Mr. Williams' youngest son was killed, which made us very sad, especially Daddy, as he had known them so well and had always packed their trunks and tuck boxes when they went to Blundells.

Food must have been difficult to get, as we had to queue for some things. As I have already mentioned, the manager at Liptons was kind to little girls, and we always got any sugar or butter if he had any. Coal was in very short supply, as we were accustomed to get it from coal boats which came in to the little port of Portreath, and they were at that time few and far between. Once one did manage to get there, but there were no coal men with carts left to distribute it, and only those who had a horse and cart of their own could get it. Fortunately our friend Mr. Nicholls had such a one and he and Daddy went down to Portreath and got a load, not a very big one because the cart wasn't very big, and Roger, the horse, could not pull a heavy load up the hills. However it was very much appreciated, I can tell you. Up to then Mother had had to make do with wood. A man whose little girl Gladys had some of my clothes had a donkey cart, (he was a road man in Mawla), and he very kindly cut up a lot of wood into little pieces which would go into the range, and Mother managed to do the cooking with them. This was a sort of forerunner of the fashionable wood-burning stoves of today, but was not so convenient in a range built for coal. This family became known to us when Daddy was in the outfitting and had a sale. In the window was a suit for a little boy, priced half a crown, and Mrs. Wills wanted to buy it for one of her children, but had not enough money to pay for it. Daddy saw her looking at it, and suggested that she should pay just sixpence and the rest whenever she could manage it. When he came home he told us about it and asked Mother if she could find some clothes for the little girl who had been with her mother (and who had been given a penny to spend, though he did not tell us that). So Mother looked through our clothes and gave some to Mrs. Wills when next she came in with her sixpence. Gladys also had one of my dolls I think. Anyway, Mrs. Wills was such a good needlewoman that when she came to see us, wearing one of Mother's frocks, Mother wished that she had been as clever. From then on the Wills family was very good to us—Mrs Wills brought us the very first blackberries the children picked, apples from their tree, eggs, (which Mother felt she could not afford to give away as she had a family to feed), and sometimes a chicken. We remained friends and still go to see Gladys, now grown up, when we go to Redruth. We could never forget how kind they were to us, and it was to Gladys that Mother gave Miss Shy Nail, and it was she who much later eased my sorrowing heart by saying, "Don't 'ee worry Miss Winnie, she was greatly loved", the most comforting words she could have spoken. From kind hearts come always the right words. Of such is truly a fleeting glimpse of the Kingdom of Heaven.

There was in the town a sort of Dad's Army, called the Volunteer Defence Corps, which Daddy joined; but I don't think it had any impact on anybody, except that its doings caused much amusement among its members.

I want to laugh nowadays when I read of schools having to be closed because a strike causes there to be no central heating.

111

We had no heating all through the war, as there was no coal to fire the boilers which were supposed to send hot water in rows of pipes to all the classrooms. We were allowed to wear an extra coat in school, and I remember having a very warm blue knitted one over which I could put my overcoat when I went outdoors. Need I add that Mother bought some very uncomfortable woollen combinations for me so that I should not catch cold. They were made by Jaegar and should have been very nice, but they tickled and I was very glad when I did manage to grow a little and they became too small, but that was alas, much later. We had to go to Camborne to school by Motor Train which we had to catch at 8.30am each morning, and at the beginning of the war, I expect due to lack of porters, the road leading to the down platform was shut and a big wooden gate locked where before we had been able to get on to the platform. Instead, we, from our end of the town, had to go under the railway arch, up Station Hill on to the Up platform, over that wretched wooden bridge, and so down to our Down platform. That took a long time and we did not like doing it. However it was solved for me by the kindly cattle dealers who also came in the train. I used to climb the gate by the wooden struts which were on the outside and one of the men would lift me over the railings. I was still very small and light so it was not so hard for them, but the bigger girls still had to go the long way round.

We were very strictly monitored when we went by train and there was a train prefect to see that we behaved properly. In those days it was considered very bad for a school girl to speak to any of the boys who came up by the train to go to the Boys' School at the other end of the town. I was once in dire disgrace through no fault of my own. I badly wanted a badge or number of anything off a uniform, and as we had no relative to supply one, Daddy asked as young soldier whom he knew if he would give me one. It happened that his younger brother went to school in Redruth, and it was arranged that he should give it to me on the platform. Daddy gave me a large apple to give to him in return, and so it was. I was amazed later in the day to be called to the Headmistress's office to give an account of myself, and though I explained, she was not satisfied until Daddy wrote a note absolving me from all intent to mix with the opposite sex. We were both about twelve years old.

We often met some very nice people in the train. Once when I was taking a bunch of roses to a favourite teacher I got in conversation with a charming man and gave him one of the roses. Imagine my surpirse when later that same day I went into the room where the French Viva was held to behold the examiner wearing my rose. I did not feel at all as if it were an examination and chatted away with ease. Wasn't that a nice thing to happen!

I remember that once a man came into town with a crate of ducks and Mr. Wicket bought them and gave Daddy two, which I thought were very nice things to have, and called them Absolam and Achitofel after Dryden's satire which I must have been studying at the time. We put them in the railed-off part of the garden, and I kept them fed and watered and became so fond of them that when the time came for us to have duck for dinner, Daddy had to take them to join their friends in Mr. Wicket's garden, so that when we did eat duck I should not know if it was either of them. Once too, someone gave Daddy a very big potato for us to have for dinner, but Daddy cut it into small pieces, each with an eye in it, and from that one potato, had a wonderful crop.

Each term Daddy had to buy me a season ticket which cost ten shillings. One day mine was lost. I remembered giving it to Mother and she put it on the mantlepiece, and then it disappeared. Daddy told Mr. Isaacs, who was the Station Master, and he gave me a new one. Many years later when Florence Paul was living in our house, she had a grate put in instead of the range, and there, behind the mantlepiece, was my ticket, a bit burned at one edge but otherwise like new. She sent it to us in Plymouth and we had many a laugh about it.

When we heard the news that the Armistice had been signed people went wild with relief, and we went down to the shop and sat in the big window, upstairs (it's still there in Rumbe-low's shop), and watched all that was going on. Several people had balloons and one lady let hers go, and there was much more fuss made about that than anything else, so although it sounds strange the memory of that balloon sailing away and

113

the woman's consternation is my most vivid remembrance of one of the most momentous days on the history of the world.

It is not strange how little things stick in one's memory whilst so many more important things get forgotten. It goes to show how very personal our memories are to us. It is only human nature after all, and we are all human though some are better humans than others. To me the worst thing about those years was not having those beautiful red leather bound books about which I have written already in 'Education'.

Clothes

MOST people will have seen pictures of little girls wearing the frocks and pinafores in which they were dressed in the early 1900s, but not everyone realises the number of garments which we wore underneath. First I must remind you that there were no man-made fabrics and no crease-resisting materials, so that there was indeed much ironing to be done by our long-suffering mothers. We had cotton, linen, silk and wool, each with different weaves and thickness so that there was always a plentiful choice when a new garment was made usually depending on the depth of one's parents' purse. Mine were fortunate in this as Daddy was the manager of the Outfittings and Tailoring Dept. of an old-established business where the Drapery Dept. was looked after by the owner, Mr. Edward Williams (the Outfitting Dept building was sold to a Bank and the Drapery building is now Rumbelows). Mother could always buy me the nicest clothes, or the material with which to make them herself, as she was very handy with her needle.

Very young babies were dressed in clothes exactly like those I have described worn by Leslie, my baby doll. After a few months all children, boys and girls were 'Tucked' their clothes being very like the long robes which they were wearing, but cut much shorter. Little bootees of silk or wool were added to keep their uncovered toes warm. So you see that there was still a lot of work for our mothers to do and those who had little sons were very glad when they could dispense with 'Nappies' and be put into small pants, and were what was called 'Britched'. Even after this milestone in their lives many little boys still kept their hair, especially if it was curly. This made the youngsters cross and they usually managed to walk around with their hands in their pockets keeping the front of their pinnies up to show their trousers. At last the curls had to go and many were the wails of woe from their mothers, and many curls saved and

115

Author showing frills and flounces.

put in a safe place for the mothers to gloat over in secret, whilst bewailing the shorn heads of their little sons. If you have read an illustrated copy of 'Little Lord Fauntleroy' you will know exactly how many little boys were dressed on Sundays or on any special occasion. My husband suffered this indignity and has told me that not until his older brother almost shamed his Mother into agreeing to let him go to the barbers did he begin to look like a real boy. Gone was the best velvet suit and the curls and he could hold his head up amongst his fellows. Little girls when out of babyhood still had many garments to put on every day and did so for several years, usually until they revolted and removed a garment surreptitiously, or went to a school where they were required to wear uniform. First came a woollen vest, mine always had sleeves and came from the Outfitting Dept as these were thicker and Mother was always afraid that I should catch cold. In spite of all her care I managed to get bronchitis every Winter, so she need not have loaded me with so many heavy garments. Over the vest came a 'Stays' (Later being replaced by a Liberty Bodice, much more comfortable). The Stays were very stiff, a foretaste of corsets to come I suppose. They were made of grey cotton much quilted and overstitched, and had adjustable shoulder straps to allow

116

for growth, so mine were never altered and the buttons remained in their original button holes until the garment wore out. There were numerous buttons all down the front to which could be attached the calico knickers about which I have told you in the article about sewing in school. The front portion remained in situ until we undressed but the back had to be able to be lowered when necessary and it was a milestone in a little girl's life when she could manage this operation by herself. It wasn't easy until little fingers learned to do one's bidding. Next came a flannel petticoat on a cotton bodice more buttons. The hem was usually embroidered and scalloped, according to one's mother's ability with a needle, or indeed her time. Over this came a cotton petticoat even more embroidered or even trimmed with lace or crochet, again depending on one's mother's clever fingers. In the bodice of each of these garments tucks were inserted to allow for growth. Need I add that mine had never to be unpicked, as the garment wore out before I grew tall enough to need their lengthening. The outermost garment was made of some woollen material in the Winter with always a blue velvet best frock for Sundays etc. and a silk one decorated with smocking for Summer days, which we seemed to be sure of at that time. I have a photo of myself wearing a silk one and very pretty it is. All buttons in those days were of linen for everyday clothes and Mother-of-Pearl for best. Plastic had not been invented and linen ones could go through the rollers in the mangle but clothes with pearl buttons had to be washed and wrung out by hand. When I was old enough to go to Trewirgie School Mr. Paul who was the Cutter in the Shop made me a beautiful navy serge kilt with many pleats which would swing out when I turned and many were the twirls I gave it as I was so proud of it. The girls in the Tailoring room made it up for me, with the inevitable cotton bodice and it lasted me all through that school, and university for Physical Education and ended up on the back of one of the girls I later taught. I was sorry to say 'Goodbye' to it old friend as it was. This was one garment where the tucks were unpicked. Over this in Winter I wore a little boys' jersey as they had high necks I did not have much interest in my clothes and so do not remember a lot about them. This was just as well as in those

117

days we had no say in the matter. As in other things we did as we were told and did not expect to have any say in the matter.

In Winter my coat was like a sailor's greatcoat, brass buttons and all, and in Spring it was succeeded by a reefer jacket also made in Shop. Mother ought to have had a little boy to clothe, but she had to do her best with me, which was difficult as I was a very feminine little girl, and looked it in spite of the boys' clothes. In Winter I wore a Man-o' War hat and in Summer a sailor's straw one of which I was secretly proud as it had a hat-band with the name of a real ship on it, but the elastic under my chin was most uncomfortable which somewhat mitigated the pride. At Easter we all went into reefer jackets or costumes if we were bigger, and at Whitsuntide no self-respecting mother would let her little girls go to church in anything but white muslin with many frills and lace and horrid cotton gloves, which I hated as they made my hands feel as if a file was being grated and gave me shivers all over. When small we wore little white cotton socks in Summer and woollen ones in Winter, but were soon promoted to long black ribbed woollen stockings held up by buttons on the Stays. Boys had elastic garters but Mother thought these were unhealthy so I had suspenders when the stockings and stays didn't meet. My footwear was always most carefully chosen, as both Mother and Daddy had painful corns due to wearing badly-fitting shoes and boots when growing, so they made up their minds that I should never suffer in this way so I had shoes and later boots made of soft leather with plenty of room for me to wriggle my toes. They had square toes and were made by a firm called Daniel Neal and the trade name was Phat-Pheet. I don't think they are made today but there are other firms who measure children's feet and make sure that the shoes fit properly. This is very expensive as most children's feet grow very quickly. It was a good thing that my feet kept pace with my body and my shoes were always worn out before I needed a bigger size. I am always grateful to my parents for their care as I have never had a corn or any other thing wrong with my feet and when we were younger my husband and I hiked miles and miles. At first the little boots were done up with tiny buttons but this caused me no trouble as Daddy always did them up for

118

me, using a silver-handled button-hook which I still have, the sole remaining part of a silver dressing-table set of which the other parts are gone. Later I was promoted to what were called 'High top boots' done up with laces, and again Daddy did them up for me each day when I was getting ready for school, and I managed them myself in school where we wore soft slippers so as not to scratch the polished floors. This was when I had passed the 'Scholarship' and went to Camborne County School at the advanced age of just eleven. Then came a great change in my clothing. We had to wear uniform, a pleated tunic over a white blouse and dark knickers instead of our white ones. Mother made me wear the white ones under the others, but these were more in the nature of linings and did not have to be so much frilled and embroided. We also had to change my kilt for the tunic and again Mr. Paul came to my aid and made me a beautiful tunic with pleats which never came out and, like the kilt, lasted me through school and University. To make sure that I should not catch cold I had to wear woollen blouses in Winter and cotton ones in Summer. I believe the woollen ones were made of Vyella which had just come on the market and the cotton ones of a specially woven material called Tobrolco. I somehow managed to get each one very dirty, in spite of trying to be clean so poor Mother had to give me a clean one every day, more washing and ironing. When the weather was wet, as it so often is in our balmy Duchy, I must have had a succession of waterproof garments but I remember only one and that because I was inordinately proud of it, and nobody else had anything like it boys' clothes again. It was a yellow oiler and Sou-Wester like the seamen and fisherman wear. It was the envy of all my friends and lasted years and years. So there was an advantage of not growing as I should. There was however one coat which I can never forget, try as I may. It was made in the Dressmaking room of beautiful blue face-cloth and had real jet buttons. It was my pride and joy, the first garment other than the Oiler that I had shown any interest in. Of course it lasted for Sunday Best for a number of years but at last it had to descend to being worn to school. Then came the tragedy. We went from Redruth to Camborne by train usually it was in a steam Motor Train but on this occasion we were coming home

119

in a proper train, carriages pulled by a real puffer which we much preferred as we could see it coming along from Gwinear Road and had time to run over the bridge if we were a bit late. Three of us were alone in one compartment and someone suggested that we could climb up onto the string luggage rack. As I was the smallest I was to go first. It seemed easy and so it was climbing up but when I came to get down one of my buttons caught in the mesh of the rack and got torn off. So good was the sewing that a piece of the cloth came off too. I was very worried and almost in tears wondering how I was to explain to Mother so as not to get punished for tearing my coat and also for being so naughty as to climb in the train. I must have thought out some explanation which Mother believed and I was punished. I thought this was an end of it but much worse was to follow. Daddy must have heard about it, and when he came home from Shop he looked at me sadly and said, "I didn't think my little girl would ever tell a lie." That was enough. The flood gates were opened, and I sobbed my heart out in his arms. But it is said that 'out of evil cometh good', and so it was. I have never since told a real lie, white ones, so as not to hurt anyone's feelings, but never a real bad one; certainly not one to get me out of difficulties. I don't believe I could. I should think I was letting Daddy down. That is still a dreadful thing to think about.

Mother was for ever having to mend the holes which I got in my long black stockings. All round the school grounds were strewn granite chippings, and I seemed to fall down far too often. I must have been clumsy, or perhaps I really could not see where I was going as I was shortsighted. Anyway, one day I foolishly remarked that the darn was not as neat as she usually made them, with the result that she said, "Then you had better darn them yourself" and so it was, and I expect I was much more careful not to fall down after that.

I had a lot of long straight hair which was plaited into either one, or sometimes two, pigtails to keep it out of the way; as Mother was afraid that I should get 'Things' in my hair as very many children in school did, and she industriously used a small-tooth comb on it nightly, not a pleasant thing to endure. However on Sundays, or for parties, I wanted to have Curls; so on Saturday nights, after I had been bathed in front of the kitchen fire, and my hair had been washed in disinfectant soap and rubbed dry (not always a pleasant proceeding as Mother stood no nonsense about soap getting in my eyes or gently easing out any tangles). Mother rolled my hair up in silk curl rags, which were most uncomfortable to lie on, but as the French say, "One must suffer to be beautiful" and the discomfort had to be put up with if I wanted to sport those curls. Daddy liked them too, so I had a special reason for suffering the rags. If the weather was fine I could go out in all my glory, but if it was damp, as it so often is in the far South West, all my efforts had been in vain; as the curls came out far more quickly than they had been put in. I hated my hair done, as there seemed always to be tangles, and I soon learned not to put my hand up near the brush as Mother was very handy with the back of it.

I don't seem to remember a lot about my clothes as I was not encouraged to be very interested in them, as we were not expected to have any say in their choice. But I do remember that Mother and Daddy always wanted me to look nice, and I do 'mind' that we all had 'best' clothes which were taken off as soon as we returned from Church, and we wore our ordinary ones until it was time to go to Sunday School, when the performance had to be repeated, and again before Church in the evening. We also had 'second best' clothes, ones which had been supplanted by the latest 'best' ones, and for school or playing we had yet another set older than the others. When trying to remember my clothes I think of the last lines of a little verse about little girls' garments. "Grandma says, 'She should be dressed in everything of the best, but very neat and plain'". I think Mother must have thought this, too, as I seem to remember that frills and furbelows must have been frowned on, as all my garments were indeed 'neat and plain. Too elaborate things were thought, 'Common'.

Cornish people say 'mind' when they mean 'remember'. Indeed they usually say, "I'd mind" which immediately leads the listener into the right state of mind, as he is inclined to try to remember if he, too, can 'mind' the same thing. Daddy was very fond of 'minding' occasions, and once when we were out for a walk with a very old gentleman and Daddy began to 'mind', the old man said, "Well, my boy, that was before my time" which made us all laugh. But it is very easy to think one can actually remember happenings which have been described to us over and over again. To me 'mind' is much more 'telling' than the more grammatical 'remember', but then to me all Cornish dialect expressions are more explicit than the usual ones.

Anyway I seem to have had the correct clothes, and happily wore what was provided, though I made them far dirtier than Mother thought possible. I think I must have been a sore disappointment to her. I could never see why she worried because I grew so slowly. Being small never worried me, but it did her. She said to me, "I don't know what we are going to do with you. You are too short to be a school teacher, and it would be no use sending you down to shop with your Daddy, you couldn't see over the counter." Poor Mother! Daddy didn't mind. The only criteria he set was that I should do something where it didn't rain on Fridays. This was because Fridays was Redruth Market Day and the farmers who drove their traps in to market brought their wives with them, and they came into shop, to buy clothes etc. But if it rained the ladies stayed at home and little business was done.

But everything turned out for the best. I grew enough to be a teacher, so Mother was satisfied. So was Daddy, but he would not have minded any way as long as I was happy and good. Bless him.